THE ANGLICAN ROSARY

JENNY LYNN ESTES

THEOPHANY
PRESS

Theophany Press
2821 Rio Linda Dr.
Bakersfield, CA 93305
theophanypress.com

© 2019 Jenny Lynn Estes

All rights reserved. No part of this book may be reproduced in any form without written permission from Theophany Press.

Most Scripture references, unless otherwise indicated, are taken from *The Holy Bible*, English Standard Version (ESV) © 2001 by Crossway, a publishing ministry of Good News Publishers. All rights reserved.

The Daily Office Scriptures and collects are from the ACNA Book of Common Prayer 2019. The Psalms are from the New Coverdale Psalter, an update of the 1535 psalter found with the first Book of Common Prayer 1549. http://anglicanchurch.net/?/main/texts_for_common_prayer

Cover Design: Front—R.L. Sather
            Back & Spine—Cynthia Bermudez & Jenny Estes
Press Logo: Zoe De Liss
Fig. 1: Jenny Estes
Rosary Diagram: Lori Lovelady

ISBN 978-1-7339710-2-7

Library of Congress Control Number: 2020275960

Printed in the United States of America

To my loving husband and soul mate

Jack Estes

You gave me the courage to put my passion on paper

Contents

Introduction 1
1 The Anglican Rosary 5
      Origin 6
      Symbology 8
      Basic Instructions 9
2 The Lord's Prayer 13
      The Lord's Prayer Rosary 19
3 The Daily Office 22
      Morning Prayer I 24
      Midday Prayer I 29
      Evening Prayer I 32
      Compline I 36
      Morning Prayer II 39
      Midday Prayer II 43
      Evening Prayer II 46
      Compline II 50
      Morning Prayer III 53
      Midday Prayer III 57
      Evening Prayer III 60
      Compline III 64
      Morning Prayer IV 67
      Midday Prayer IV 71
      Evening Prayer IV 74
      Compline IV 78
4 Holy Mysteries 81
      Joyful Mysteries 84
      Sorrowful Mysteries 88
      Glorious/Luminous Mysteries 92
5 A.C.T.S Prayer 96
      A.C.T.S. Rosary 99
6 St. Patrick's Breastplate 103
      St. Patrick's Breastplate Rosary 105
7 The Way of the Cross 108
      Way of the Cross Rosary I 110
      Way of the Cross Rosary II 114
      Way of the Cross Rosary III 118
8 Lectio Divina 122
      Lectio Divina Rosary 125
9 Daily Scripture Readings 128
      Daily Scripture Rosary 130
Lectionary Year One 132
Lectionary Year Two 145
Acknowledgments 159
References 160

Introduction

*True prayer is neither a mere mental exercise nor a vocal performance.
It is far deeper than that - it is spiritual transaction
with the Creator of Heaven and Earth.*
—Charles Spurgeon

Multi-colored beads and crosses caught my attention as I walked into the regional Daughters of the King meeting. One of the members was offering Rosaries she made for sale. I'd never heard of an Anglican Rosary but was fascinated enough to buy one. The ruby red beads and Celtic cross called to me, but I had no idea what to do with them.

When I got home, I ordered every book I could find regarding the Anglican Rosary (or Protestant Prayer Beads). Research turned into experimentation which turned into joy, then intense longing. Using the Rosary to pray and meditate deepened my connection to God and helped me stay focused for longer periods of time. The beads became an anchor for stillness, and my heart opened to the stirrings of the Holy Spirit. However, I quickly became frustrated with the simple forms and methods for using the Rosary that were available—I wanted more structure and depth.

One morning I sat with the Rosary in my hands and wondered if I could use it with the Lord's Prayer. As my fingers moved through the cycle of beads, the familiar petitions fell into place and came alive. I felt God's presence as I worshiped his name and sought his guidance, help, and strength. Filled with hope, I pondered what other methods of prayer and meditation might be enhanced through use with the Rosary.

Hence, this book.

Most of us find it difficult to come away from the distractions and stresses of everyday life to spend time with God. With so many concerns and wandering minds, we find it hard to trust and find peace as we pray. Using the Rosary changes everything. No matter what circumstances we find ourselves in, the Rosary can immediately draw us into a quiet state of being. The simple act of holding the beads becomes an anchor for peace and attunes our hearts to God's purposes and provision.

The wonder of the Rosary is it engages our entire being. Our minds and hearts are set free to pay attention to what God is revealing to us in the present moment. This makes us more sensitive to his movements throughout our day. Increased awareness of his presence reminds us we are not alone on our journey through this life.

The Anglican Rosary is an invaluable tool for people of faith to deepen their connection with God. Also known as Anglican Prayer Beads, or the Protestant Rosary, this simple combination of cross and numbered beads richly symbolizes Christ's own journey on earth. We are drawn into his presence as we meditate on the mysteries of our Christian faith.

The difference between Catholic and Anglican Rosaries is found in the number of beads and the form of prayers. While the Catholic Rosary is prayed with a focus on Mary for help in contemplating the mysteries of Jesus' life; the Anglican Rosary relies on the Holy Spirit to guide and enhance times of prayer, worship, and encounter with Scripture.

My life has been enriched and transformed through a deeper understanding and connection to classic and liturgical forms of prayer that I've adapted for personal use with the Rosary. I am blessed to be able to share them with you in this book. Based on Holy Scripture, these forms of prayer have been the foundation of spiritual life since the beginning of Christendom. When used with the Rosary they come alive in the present moment because we are fully engaged—body, soul, and spirit—in prayer and communion with God.

Introduction

The Anglican Rosary is a lifeline of faith reaching out to connect with the heart of our Creator. It will enhance your quiet times and enrich your meditations. So take this journey with me and get to know God—Father, Son, and Holy Spirit—as the One who is ever available, always present, and ready to listen.

Jenny Lynn Estes

~1~
The Anglican Rosary

The practice of silence throws off the ego and allows the mind and heart to attend to God on his terms, not our own.
—*Deacon Leslie Arbegast*

When we sit quietly in the presence of God something happens. Desires pour forth, fears subside, and a supernatural calm floods our being. *Easy for you to say,* you might think. And I would answer *yes*—because praying with a Rosary opened the door to God's presence in my life.

The more I use the Rosary in my devotional times, the easier it is to enter into a quiet state of being. That's because the Rosary has become an anchor for stillness. As soon as I touch the beads my body relaxes, my mind quiets, and my heart opens.

The purpose of the Rosary is to connect and to listen. Though we are repeating phrases, we are fully engaged. Our hearts yield to God and our minds open to inspiration from the Holy Spirit. When I lead Rosary workshops I tell participants if they find themselves evaluating their experience while attempting to pray—*I'm not doing this right, I don't get it, I don't feel anything*—they are in their heads instead of their hearts. They need to focus on the words and recite the phrases out loud (even if under their breath). Speaking the words out loud shuts down the critical mind. Only when our internal voice is silenced can we truly listen.

Prayer cannot be rushed. It takes time to slow down enough to be receptive to the Holy Spirit. The Rosary uses repetition as a form of meditation in similar ways as the Psalms. When Jesus forbade meaningless repetition[1], he was referring to vain and empty phrases. God is not impressed by a waterfall of words. Any prayer can be empty and meaningless if our thoughts are a million miles away and we mechanically recite scripture. Praying with beads in a deliberate and meditative way invites the kind of focused intentionality that God honors.

Origins

The first Christians to use beads with their prayers were in the Irish community of St. Colomba in the ninth century. Though the practice of using stones and knots to count prayers originated with the Desert Fathers and Mothers in the third century, it was the Irish that exchanged their knotted strings for the texture and beauty of beads. Interestingly, the word "bead" comes from the Anglo-Saxon word "bede," which means "to pray or request." The practice of praying and meditating with beads quickly spread throughout Europe.

St. Benedict, the founder of monastic living, believed reciting Scripture daily was foundational to prayer and right relationship with God. In the Middle Ages, Benedictine monks used strings of one hundred and fifty beads to pray through the psalms each week. To help the illiterate laity engage in the practice, the psalms were replaced with the Lord's Prayer. The "Our Father," or "Pater Noster" in Latin, could be easily memorized and was a powerful prayer for repetition. These strings of beads soon became known as the Paternoster and were popular among the faithful, rich and poor alike.

St. Dominic received a vision from the Virgin Mary in the year 1214 which manifested as the Catholic Rosary. He spent the remainder of his life spreading the practice of this new devotion. The Rosary encouraged meditating on the mysteries of Jesus Christ's life, death, and resurrection. Many miracles have been attributed to praying this Rosary, and it continues to be a vibrant and essential part of Catholic worship today.

---

[1] Matthew 6:7

During the Reformation when Martin Luther separated from the Catholic church (the beginning of Protestantism), he continued to promote the Rosary as a form of devotion. However, because it included the veneration of Mary, use of the Catholic Rosary rapidly diminished among Protestants.

Then in the 1980s a Texas study group exploring different forms of prayer became excited about embracing the focus of the Rosary while using Protestant symbols. And thus, the Anglican Rosary was birthed. With its symbology based on the life of Jesus, the thirty-three beads and cross mirror our connection with God Incarnate, as well as the spiritual and elemental rhythms and seasons here on earth.

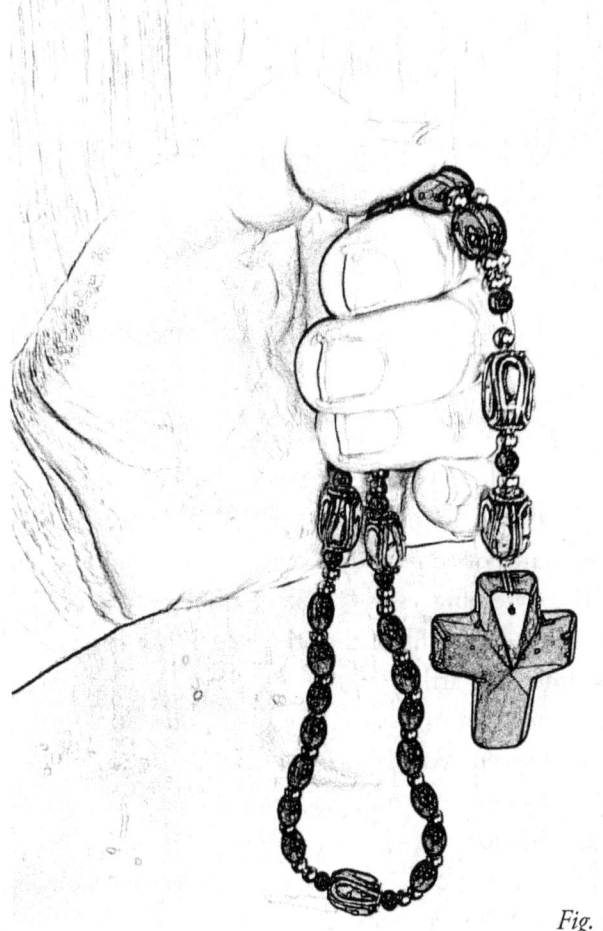

Fig. 1

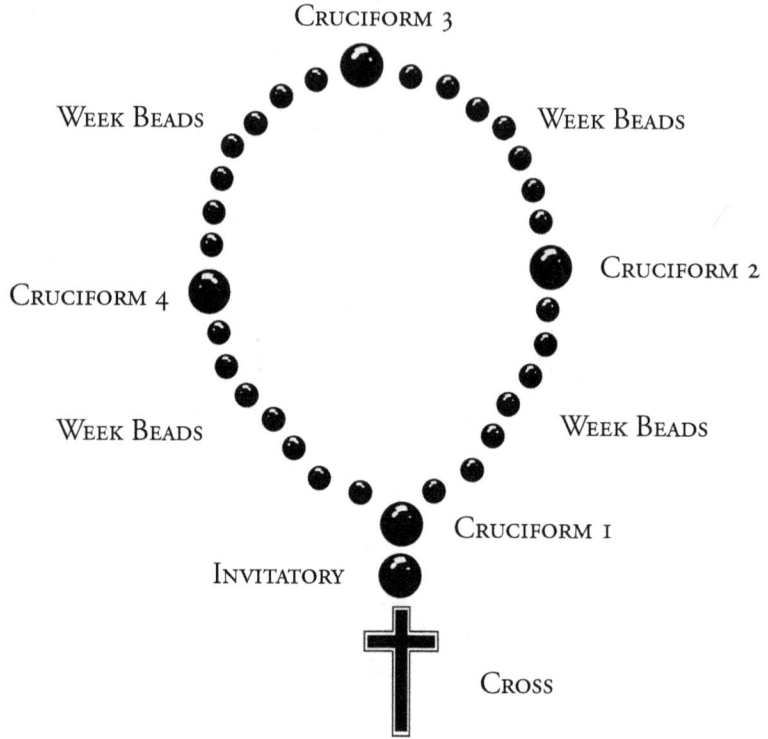

Symbology

The Anglican Rosary beautifully illustrates Christian faith and tradition. The thirty-three beads, representing Christ's life on earth, are linked together in a circular manner that begins and ends on the cross. Jesus, the source of faith, is our beginning and end. The circular nature of the Rosary embraces the sense of wholeness found in deep relationship with God. It is likened to the wheel of time symbolizing our spiritual journey on earth.

The Rosary consists of one Invitatory bead, four Cruciform beads and four groups of seven Week beads, as illustrated above.

The Cross represents the saving grace of God acting in our lives to bring us into his kingdom.

The Invitatory bead is our entrance into prayer and worship. We place ourselves in the presence of God and open our hearts to receive his Word.

The four Cruciform beads form the shape of a cross and remind us that Christ is central in our lives. The number four also symbolizes the following:

The cardinal virtues: Prudence, Justice, Fortitude, and Temperance. Representing the moral foundation of all humanity.

The essential elements of life: Earth, Air, Fire, and Water. Everything we need for survival on this planet.

The points of the compass: North, South, East, and West. Provides direction and location.

The seasons of the year: Summer, Winter, Spring, and Fall. Mirror our time on earth.

The seven Week beads follow each Cruciform. There are four sets of seven beads. The number seven stands for spiritual completeness, or perfection. The Week beads recall the seven days of creation; the days of the week; the seasons of the liturgical year; and the seven sacraments of the church.

We join with God through prayer and worship to receive spiritual sustenance to live in a way that glorifies him, blesses us, and bears fruit for the world.

Basic Instructions for using a Rosary

Place the written Rosary you want to pray on a table in front of you, or in your lap. Open your left hand as if you were reaching for a handshake. Drape the Rosary beads over your left fingers with the cross and a few beads hanging over your knuckles. Make a light fist around the beads, using your thumb and forefinger to secure the Rosary (see Fig. 1 on page 7). Now grasp the cross with your right thumb and forefinger. You may rest both hands in your lap as you pray or hold them up as you move through the beads.

Pray the words under the Cross heading of the Rosary. Then move your thumb and forefinger to the Invitatory Bead. Now recite the prayer under the Invitatory heading. When finished, move to the first Cruciform bead and do the same.

The next portion will be the seven Week beads on the right of the circle of beads. As you move to the first Week bead, allow the bottom half of the circle of beads to drop around your left hand so you are just holding the beads you are ready to pray with. Using your thumbs and forefingers on both hands, move forward one bead at a time, repeating the phrase for that section on each of the seven beads.

Hold the 2nd Cruciform bead with your right thumb and forefinger and pray the prayer attached to it. When finished move through the next seven Week beads as before, reciting the new refrain while meditating on the Cruciform reading.

Continue in this way until you come to the end of the fourth set of Week beads (the completion of the circle). At this point your hands will have reversed, with the left thumb and forefinger holding the 1st Cruciform and the circle of beads draped over the right hand.

To finish the Rosary, move your right thumb and forefinger to 1st Cruciform, then the Invitatory bead, then the Cross—praying the words attached to each section—ending up with the entire Rosary in your right hand.

Holding and praying with a Rosary is very individual. Once you understand the basic idea, you can hold, move and interact with the Rosary in whatever way is natural to you. Some keep Rosaries in their pockets at work and will finger them throughout the day to stay mindful of God's presence. Others are able to hold and pray with small Rosaries using only one hand. One young man I know sleeps with a Rosary under his pillow to ward off recurring nightmares and calm his anxiety.

How to Pray a Rosary

Written Rosaries are laid out in a pattern that follows the order of the beads shown in the diagram on page 8. Every Rosary begins on the Cross, moves up to the Invitatory bead, the first Cruciform, then to the right of the loop with the next seven Week beads, and so on.

Each of the beads has specific prayers, phrases, or Scriptures attached to it. Different Rosaries may have extra instructions for each section, but the basic format is to pray the designated words out loud, and from your heart. Mindless, automatic recitation has no place here. The point of using a Rosary is to engage fully in this time with God.

While repeating the assigned phrase on each of the Week beads, you will meditate, or contemplate on what you just read on the previous Cruciform. This is the time to listen and allow the Holy Spirit to interact with you. Don't rush the Week beads.

All the Rosaries in this book start and end on the Cross, though what you say out loud will differ with each one. Many of them begin with the *sign of the cross*, which is a form of blessing or crossing oneself that places us in God's hands. Praying the sign of the cross puts our minds and thoughts on God, centers our hearts and feelings on Jesus, and penetrates our souls with grace. This beautiful gesture can be included in your worship by holding the cross of the Rosary in your right hand and doing the following:

> Touch the cross to your forehead as you say,
> "In the name of the Father…"
> Touch the cross to your heart, "the Son…"
> Touch the cross first to the front of your left shoulder,
>   then right shoulder saying, "and the Holy Spirit."
> Touch your heart again as you end with, "Amen."

How to Stay Focused

One of the key benefits of using a Rosary is the ability to stay focused throughout your prayer time. As you hold the beads and pray out loud while thinking about the scripture just read, there's no room for distracting thoughts. When first learning to pray this way, you may find yourself judging the experience instead of meditating. If that happens, simply refocus on the scripture, and on listening to the Holy Spirit. Pray from your heart.

It's important to recite Scripture and prayers out loud. This helps your mind focus and allows the Holy Spirit to interact with you.

Vocal prayer and worship immerses us in God's presence and prepares us to receive from him.

Opening Your Heart

To open your heart means to surrender your agenda for this time of prayer and to humbly present yourself before God—ready and willing to receive from him. Praying from your heart is an offering up of all cares and concerns to God with confidence, yet without demand—like children, secure in their parent's love, ask for help.

God is always with us, but we are so distracted by the world, and our concerns, we often feel disconnected and alone. The Rosary is a tool to engage our entire being in prayer, worship, and meditation. With use over time, it becomes an anchor for awareness of God's presence in our lives. Praying with the Rosary keeps our hearts receptive to the Holy Spirit and helps us see the world through God's eyes. His strength, guidance, and peace are available in any given moment. Learning to be present with the Rosary prepares us to be present with God regardless of our state of being.

Final Thoughts

The key to praying with a Rosary is time. Setting aside a quiet place and time to pray is essential. Once you are familiar with using a Rosary, that time may only be ten minutes—but those ten minutes of focused listening will be far more beneficial and rewarding than twenty minutes of distracted, disconnected prayer, and hurried scripture reading.

In the beginning, it's best to have uninterrupted time to learn how to pray and meditate with a Rosary. The more you use one, the easier it will be to find a calm and receptive state of being to engage with God's Word.

~2~
The Lord's Prayer

Prayer lays hold of God's plan and becomes the link between His will and its accomplishment on earth. Amazing things happen, and we are given the privilege of being the channels of the Holy Spirit's prayer.
— Elisabeth Elliot

The Lord's Prayer is the prayer we know by heart. We say it together in church and use it to conclude times of fellowship. It's our go-to prayer when time is short or when we find ourselves in crisis. Although we honor God each time we recite it, Jesus never meant it to be used as a simple repetitive prayer.

When the disciples asked Jesus to teach them to pray, it was because they saw the transformational effect of prayer in him. Unlike the hundreds of prayers they recited in the temple and heard priests pray out loud, Jesus' prayers invoked the life-changing power of the Holy Spirit. The disciples marveled at the intimacy Jesus shared with his Father, and witnessed the resulting power throughout his ministry. They wanted to experience God in the same way Jesus did—just as we long for a deeper connection with him today.

Jesus encourages us to come away from the distractions of the world and to commune with God in private. The model prayer he gave the disciples is a beautiful pattern for transformative living and worship. The six petitions of the Lord's prayer embrace each important aspect of Christian faith. Praying this way honors the sovereignty of God and acknowledges his continued presence in our world. Here we find hope for the future, protection from evil, and intercede for a world in pain and need.

The Lord's Prayer includes six petitions that encompass who God is and our relationship to him. The first three petitions remind us that worship is primary in our interaction with God. Praise and thanksgiving are the entry points that align our hearts and wills with his, bringing us into close communion with him.

The next three petitions encapsulate what is necessary for our lives here on earth. We ask provision for daily needs, seek forgiveness for the many ways we fall short, and cry out for protection from evil that would harm and lead us astray.

To conclude we return to praise, affirming our faith and affixing our hope on the living God. With confidence we move through life, spirits uplifted, secure our relationship with our Father.

Let's take a closer look at the individual petitions.

Our Father, who art in heaven

This is the foundation for prayer. Belief in God and the resurrection of Jesus Christ opens the way for us to approach the Creator of the universe as "Our Father". Jesus repeatedly addressed God as "Father" in the New Testament which was a huge departure from Jewish tradition. As the Son of God, the way he prayed highlighted the intimate relationship Jesus had with his Father. His death and resurrection then paved the way for us as adopted children to approach God in the same manner. God is not only our Creator but through Jesus' redemptive work he is our Father.

Though infinitely powerful, all-knowing, and transcendent—we are free to approach God as little children, secure in his love and mercy, confident in his desire to help us. Earthly fathers fail in so many ways, but our Father in heaven will not. God is the perfect Father who embodies all the good that fatherhood represents. In return, we owe him our absolute respect, love, and honor.

We begin this first petition by humbly placing ourselves in his presence. Though he transcends this world, he cares for us with a Father's heart and is ready to listen when we come to him in prayer.

His love is unconditional and constant. His discipline is timely and appropriate. Let us approach our Father in heaven with reverence and awe, secure in the knowledge that he understands and cares about the deepest desires of our hearts.

Hallowed by thy name

Hallow means to "honor as holy." God is separate from his creation. He is infinitely pure. In order to approach him, we must believe in his eternal presence and power. By hallowing his name we put ourselves in the proper attitude to petition him.

Throughout Scripture, people honored God's name when he helped them in their time of need. Hagar praised him as El Ro'i, the God who sees when he rescued her in the wilderness. Abraham called him Yahveh Yir'eh, God will provide, in thanksgiving for the ram sacrificed in Issac's place. When the Israelites were miraculously delivered from enemies ravaging their settlements, Gideon built an altar to honor Yahveh Shalom, the Lord is Peace. They worshiped him through glorifying his name and the many aspects of his character.

We hallow God's name for the diverse ways he intercedes and interacts in our lives. His presence brings transformation and healing to all who regard him as holy. Worshipping God by hallowing his name unites us with the Holy Spirit so our prayers flow directly from our hearts to his.

Thy kingdom come, thy will be done,
on earth as it is in heaven

This petition moves us from worshipping God into praying for his kingdom to expand on earth. God's will is gloriously and joyously done in heaven. As his children on earth, we have the privilege, if not the responsibility, to respond to his love by living lives that seek his honor and promote the gospel of Jesus Christ. When we embrace the sovereignty of God by trusting him regardless of circumstances, his kingdom continues to grow in and through us.

Jesus modeled the integration of heaven and earth perfectly. His ministry changed the world. We join with him in prayer that nothing would hinder the expansion of God's kingdom and the fulfillment of all his promises.

When we pray "Thy will be done," the power of the Holy Spirit releases God's purpose in our lives. We seek God's glory in all we pray for—and accept his will in every answer.

Give us this day our daily bread

Here we are encouraged to offer up specific needs of our own, and for others. As we pray to Almighty God who is willing and able to provide for us, we are reminded that we depend on him for more than just material needs like food, clothing, and shelter. This is where we find grace to face difficulties on a daily basis, and strength to move forward in the direction he leads. We ask for healing for ourselves and others, and we thank God for everything he has already provided.

Life is uncertain, but God never changes. We come to him for that which we need today, knowing that tomorrow is in his hands. We invite him into our day, trusting he will guide us through it and provide all that is necessary for whatever needs arise.

This petition reflects our dependence on God for all of life's necessities—physical, spiritual, and emotional. We pray with thanksgiving for all he has done and is continuing to do in our lives.

Forgive us our trespasses,
as we forgive those who trespass against us

This fifth petition keeps us in good standing with God. As sojourners on this earth, we all fall short of his holiness. We are reminded of our need for confession and the kindness and love we owe others. In order to maintain a close relationship with God, we must bridge the separation that sin creates. We do that by asking for forgiveness on the basis of what Jesus accomplished on the cross, not because we deserve to be forgiven by our own merit.

Sin is caused not only through what we do but also by the good we neglect. Anytime we fail to treat others with mercy and love, we have not done what God has called us to do. This is the time to examine our hearts through the lens of the Holy Spirit and to repent. Once we express sorrow for our shortcomings, we are free to receive God's forgiveness. We thank him for his mercy and move on.

The second part of this petition pertains to our relationship with others. Scripture promises if we forgive others, our heavenly Father will forgive us. If we are to find mercy with God, we must also show mercy to others. Our forgiveness is not based upon what others do or don't do but is offered in obedience to God—the ultimate judge and arbiter. When we forgive others, we are not saying what they did was ok, we are simply letting go of the need to punish them and giving it to God. This frees us emotionally to let go of bitterness and resentment and move forward in our own lives.

Lead us not into temptation, but deliver us from evil

With this petition, we turn from past failings to future vulnerability. We ask our Father to spare us from temptation and deliver us from spiritual attacks that might lead to new sin. Satan tempts us where we are weak and vulnerable. This can cause us to act out in ways that allow sin to take root in our lives. Here we seek protection from the devil's wiles and pray that the temptations and trials God permits will not overwhelm over us.

We live in a fallen world. Sin and evil compete to keep us from God. We need the power of the Holy Spirit to overcome these trials. Jesus encourages us to ask daily to be spared from temptation. When we try to be strong in our own power it gives place to the enemy. Through prayer, we are delivered from the chains the evil one tries to bind us in. We do well to put ourselves at God's mercy.

For thine is the kingdom,
and the power, and the glory, for ever and ever

To conclude our prayer we return to worship. We praise God who has the power to accomplish all we ask for in the glory of his name. He is our Maker and our Redeemer. With confidence, we leave all cares and concerns in his capable hands. God is gracious, slow to anger, and abounding in mercy. Jesus showed us how to reach out to him through prayer. May he be magnified in this world and beyond.

Amen

So be it.

May all be fulfilled according to God's will and his Word. In faith and with confidence, having put everything into his hands, we rest in the assurance of his love.

Now that we have an understanding of the petitions in the Lord's Prayer, the next section will help us pray through it with the Rosary. This provides structure to incorporate our individual prayers into the Lord's Prayer. The Rosary grounds and guides us through each petition with the opportunity to pray personal requests and express heartfelt concerns while keeping our focus on God. The prayer beads anchor our hearts in the present moment. Our praise breaks through the darkness and connects us with the heavenly realm, where our petitions can be heard and answered.

How To Pray This Rosary

Using the diagram of the Anglican Rosary (page 8), follow the pattern for praying by beginning on the Cross. The Rosary keeps you focused on God as you pray through the petitions of the Lord's Prayer. Be sensitive to the leading of the Holy Spirit. If the Lord reveals something to you, pause, meditate, and pray about it before continuing.

Speak the petitions and your prayers out loud, or softly under your breath. Close your eyes as much as possible, allowing your fingers to move across the beads as you pray. The Weeks have suggestions for each bead, but you can pray as the Spirit leads and focus on only one or two aspects of the petition—or add your own—instead of praying through each item.

The following Rosary will help you learn to pray through the petitions of the Lord's Prayer. Eventually, you want to be able to pray spontaneously from the desires of your heart, without referring to the guide as you move through each line of the prayer.

The Lord's Prayer Rosary

Cross
Make the sign of the cross

In the name of the Father, the Son, and the Holy Spirit. Amen.

Invitatory
Place yourself in God's presence. The living God, your heavenly Father desires only good in your life. Approach him with humility and awe.

Our Father, Who art in heaven

Cruciform 1
Pray that God's Holy Name would be revered throughout the world.

Hallowed be thy name.

Week
The Names of God reflect his presence in our lives. Praise God for who he is by reciting one or more of the Names below with thanksgiving for his faithfulness.

Yahweh	Almighty, Infinite, Unchanging
Creator	Of heaven and earth
Adonai	Lord and Master
El Ro'i	God who sees me
Jehovah Jireh	The Lord who provides
Abba Father	The One who cares for me
Yahveh Shalom	The Lord is my peace

Cruciform 2
Pray for God's will and the spread of his kingdom to manifest throughout the world and in our lives.

Thy kingdom come, thy will be done, on earth as it is in heaven.

The Anglican Rosary

Week

On each bead offer up current events and concerns for the following areas; or, focus on one or more areas each day.

The World	For peace, righteous leadership, creation
Christianity	The Gospel, church, holy leadership
Your Church	Purity, leadership, growth, fellowship
Your Family	Direction, provision, salvation
Your Work	Co-workers, environment, prosperity
Your Future	Wisdom, discernment, faithfulness
Specific Situation	Guidance, understanding, help

Cruciform 3

Pray for personal concerns and needs for yourself and others which may include any, or all, of the suggestions on the Week beads. Be specific. God is able and willing to provide.

Give us this day our daily bread.

Week

Personal needs for you and your loved ones
Healing for yourself and others
Salvation for family and co-workers
Provision for emotional, spiritual, and material needs
Thanksgiving for answered prayers and future help
Concerns for the future
Grace to face difficulties; strength to move forward

Cruciform 4

Receive mercy for the times you've fallen short of love, obedience, and gratitude. Forgive others by letting go of the need to punish them and give it to God.

Forgive us our trespasses,

    as we forgive those who trespass against us.

Week

Pray using one or more of the suggestions below, or for what might be weighing your spirit down.

> Ask the Holy Spirit to reveal sin in your life
> Confess where you have fallen short or sinned
> Ask God to forgive you
> Forgive and release others
> Set your will to forgive those who sin against you
> Pray for those who have hurt you
> Forgive yourself as your Father has forgiven you

Cruciform 1

Pray for protection over yourself, your family, church, and home. Ask the Father to spare you and your loved ones from future temptation. Pray for deliverance from evil, that the enemy would have no place in your life.

> Lead us not into temptation, but deliver us from evil.

Invitatory

Return to praise and worship—thanking God who hears your prayers. He has invited you to participate in his kingdom which never ends. Give him the glory.

> For thine is the kingdom, and the power and the glory,
>   for ever and ever.

Cross

May all be fulfilled according to his will and his Word.

> Amen.

~3~
The Daily Office

In the morning, prayer is the key that opens to us the treasures of God's mercies and blessings; in the evening, it is the key that shuts us up under his protection and safeguard.
—Billy Graham

Jewish tradition includes a cycle of praying at set times throughout each day. The Apostles continued the practice with the early church. Over time, standard formats and set hours flowed into a beautiful liturgy modeled on the rhythms of life beginning with sunrise and ending with night prayer. This is called the Daily Office.

This ancient and disciplined way of marking time is a rich and accessible way of praying based on scripture. Traditionally the Daily Office is prayed in group settings with a leader guiding participants. Now, we can use this dynamic prayer form as individuals using the Rosary as a guide.

Included in this book are simplified forms of morning, noontime, evening prayer, and compline (night prayer). Each session is comprised of psalms, prayers, and collects, which are specific prayers for certain days and seasons.

This way of praying keeps one mindful of God throughout the day. It expands and organizes prayer. Many who engage in the discipline have found it life-altering. I have also found great benefit in using it periodically.

When stressed, or short on time, the Daily Office has become my go-to prayer form because I don't have to struggle with what or how long to pray. As soon as I grab my Rosary and start, I'm immediately transported into an attitude of worship, gratitude, and thanksgiving. I find comfort in the midst of present need, and courage to move forward knowing God is with me in every circumstance.

How To Pray This Rosary

Using the diagram of the Anglican Rosary (page 8), follow the pattern for praying by reciting the psalms and prayers connected to each bead in the Daily Office you are praying. The main elements of the liturgy are on the Cruciform beads. For the Week beads, you can repeat the suggested refrain or take one line from the previous reading to recite and meditate on.

The Lord's Prayer has been placed at the end of the Daily Office Rosaries to allow extended time to add personal petitions if desired.

Morning Prayer I

Cross
Psalm 19:14

> Let the words of my mouth and the meditation of my heart
>   be acceptable in your sight,
> O Lord, my rock and my redeemer.

Invitatory
Venite   Psalm 95:1-7

> O come, let us sing unto the Lord;
>   let us make a joyful noise to the rock of our salvation!
> Let us come into his presence with thanksgiving;
>   let us make a joyful noise to him with songs of praise!
> For the Lord is a great God,
>   and a great King above all gods.
> In his hand are the depths of the earth;
>   the heights of the mountains are his also.
> The sea is his, for he made it,
>   and his hands formed the dry land.
> Oh come, let us worship and bow down;
>   let us kneel before the Lord, our Maker!
> For he is our God,
>   and we are the people of his pasture,
>   and the sheep of his hand.
> O, that today you would hearken to his voice!

Cruciform 1
Te Deum Laudamus   We Praise You, O God

> We praise you, O God,
>   we acclaim you as Lord;
>   all creation worships you,
>   the Father everlasting.

To you all angels, all the powers of heaven,
The cherubim and seraphim, sing in endless praise:
   Holy, Holy, Holy, Lord God of power and might,
   heaven and earth are full of your glory.
The glorious company of apostles praise you.
The noble fellowship of prophets praise you.
The white-robed army of martyrs praise you.
Throughout the world the holy Church acclaims you:
   Father, of majesty unbounded,
   your true and only Son, worthy of all praise,
   the Holy Spirit, advocate and guide.
You, Christ, are the king of glory,
   the eternal Son of the Father.
When you took our flesh to set us free
   you humbly chose the virgin's womb.
You overcame the sting of death
   and opened the kingdom of heaven to all believers.
You are seated at God's right hand in glory.
   we believe that you will come to be our judge.
Come then, Lord, and help your people,
   bought with the price of your own blood,
   and bring us with your saints
   to glory everlasting.
Save your people, Lord, and bless your inheritance;
   govern and uphold them now and always.
Day by day we bless you;
   we praise your name forever.
Keep us today, Lord, from all sin;
   have mercy on us, Lord, have mercy.
Lord, show us your love and mercy,
   for we have put our trust in you.
In you, Lord, is our hope,
   let us never be put to shame.

WEEK

Lord, show us your love and mercy, for we put our trust in you.

CRUCIFORM 2
Prayer

> O Lord, show your mercy upon us;
> and grant us your salvation.
> O Lord, guide those who govern us;
> and lead us in the way of justice and truth.
> Clothe your ministers with righteousness;
> and let your people sing with joy.
> O Lord, save your people;
> and bless your inheritance.
> Give peace in our time, O Lord;
> and defend us by your mighty power.
> Let not the needy, O Lord, be forgotten;
> nor the hope of the poor be taken away.
> Create in us clean hearts, O God;
> and take not your Holy Spirit from us.

WEEK
Psalm 51:10

> Create in me a clean heart, O God;
> and renew a right spirit within me.

CRUCIFORM 3
Collect for Guidance

> Heavenly Father, in you we live and move and have our being: We humbly pray you so to guide and govern us by your Holy Spirit, that in all the cares and occupations of our life we may not forget you, but may remember that we are ever walking in your sight; through Jesus Christ our Lord. Amen.

WEEK

> The mercy of the Lord is everlasting: O come, let us adore him.

Cruciform 4
The General Thanksgiving

Almighty God, Father of all mercies,
> we your unworthy servants give you humble thanks
> for all your goodness and loving-kindness
> to us and to all whom you have made.

We bless you for our creation, preservation,
> and all the blessings of this life;
> but above all for your immeasurable love
> in the redemption of the world by our Lord Jesus Christ;
> for the means of grace, and for the hope of glory.

And, we pray, give us such an awareness of your mercies,
> that with truly thankful hearts we may show forth your praise,
> not only with our lips, but in our lives,
> by giving up our selves to your service,
> and by walking before you
> in holiness and righteousness all our days;

Through Jesus Christ our Lord,
> to whom, with you and the Holy Spirit,
> be honor and glory throughout all ages. Amen.

Week

The Word was made flesh and dwelt among us:
O come, let us adore him.

Cruciform 1
The Lord's Prayer

Our Father, who art in heaven,
> hallowed be thy Name,
> thy kingdom come,
> thy will be done,
>> on earth as it is in heaven.

Give us this day our daily bread.
And forgive us our trespasses,
> as we forgive those
>> who trespass against us.

And lead us not into temptation,
   but deliver us from evil.
For thine is the kingdom,
   and the power, and the glory,
   for ever and ever. Amen.

Invitatory

Romans 15:13

May the God of hope fill you with all joy and peace in believing, so that by the power of the Holy Spirit you may abound in hope.

Cross

Glory be to the Father, and to the Son, and to the Holy Spirit; as it was in the beginning, is now, and ever shall be, world without end. Amen.

Midday Prayer I

Cross
In the name of the Father, the Son, and the Holy Spirit. Amen.

Invitatory
O God, make speed to save us.
O Lord, make haste to help us.

Cruciform 1
Psalm 119:105-108

Your word is a lantern to my feet
  and a light upon my path.
I have sworn and am steadfastly purposed
  to keep your righteous judgments.
I am troubled above measure;
  revive me, O Lord, according to your word.
Let the freewill offerings of my mouth please you, O Lord,
  and teach me your judgments.

Week
Accept, O Lord, the freewill offerings of my mouth,
and teach me your judgments.

Cruciform 2
Romans 5:5

The love of God has been poured into our hearts through the Holy Spirit that has been given to us.

Week
Let Your love guide my thoughts and comfort my spirit today.

Cruciform 3

Psalm 119: 109-112

> My life is always in my hand,
>   yet I do not forget your law.
> The ungodly have laid a snare for me,
>   but I have not strayed from your commandments.
> Your testimonies have I claimed as my heritage for ever;
>   and why? They are the very joy of my heart.
> I have applied my heart to fulfill your statutes
>   even unto the end.

Week

> I have applied my heart to fulfill your statues even unto to the end.

Cruciform 4

> O Lord, you never fail to support and govern those whom you bring up in your steadfast love and fear: Keep us, we pray, under your continual protection and providence, and give us a perpetual fear and love of your holy Name; through Jesus Christ our Lord who lives and reigns with you and the Holy Spirit, one God, for ever and ever. Amen.

Week

> Lord, have mercy. Christ have mercy.

Cruciform 1

The Lord's Prayer

> Our Father, who art in heaven,
>   hallowed be thy Name,
>   thy kingdom come,
>   thy will be done,
>   on earth as it is in heaven.
> Give us this day our daily bread.
> And forgive us our trespasses,
>   as we forgive those
>   who trespass against us.
> And lead us not into temptation,
>   but deliver us from evil.

For thine is the kingdom,
>   and the power, and the glory,
>   for ever and ever. Amen.

INVITATORY

Almighty Savior, who at midday called your servant Saint Paul to be an apostle to the Gentiles: We pray you to illumine the world with the radiance of your glory, that all nations may come and worship you; for you live and reign with the Father and the Holy Spirit, one God, for ever and ever. Amen.

CROSS

Glory be to the Father, and to the Son, and to the Holy Spirit; as it was in the beginning, is now, and ever shall be, world without end. Amen.

Evening Prayer I

Cross

John 8:12

> Jesus spoke to them, saying, "I am the light of the world. Whoever follows me will not walk in darkness, but will have the light of life."

Invitatory

Phos hilaron   O Gladsome Light

> O gladsome light,
> pure brightness of the everliving Father in heaven,
>   O Jesus Christ, holy and blessed!
> Now as we come to the setting of the sun,
> and our eyes behold the vesper light,
>   we sing your praises, O God: Father, Son, and Holy Spirit.
> You are worthy at all times to be praised by happy voices,
>   O Son of God, O Giver of Life,
>   and to be glorified through all the worlds.

Cruciform 1

Surge, illuminare   Arise, shine, for your light has come

Isaiah 60:1-3, 11a, 14c, 18-19

> Arise, shine, for your light has come,
>   and the glory of the Lord has dawned upon you.
> For behold, darkness covers the land;
>   deep gloom enshrouds the peoples.
> But over you the Lord will rise,
>   and his glory will appear upon you.
> Nations will stream to your light,
>   and kings to the brightness of your dawning.
> Your gates will always be open;
>   by day or night they will never be shut.
> They will call you, The City of the Lord,
>   the Zion of the Holy One of Israel.
> Violence will no more be heard in your land,
>   ruin or destruction within your borders.

Evening Prayer I

> You will call your walls, Salvation,
>   and all your portals, Praise.
> The sun will no more be your light by day;
>   by night you will not need the brightness of the moon.
> The Lord will be your everlasting light,
>   and your God will be your glory.

Week
Psalm 141:2

> Let my prayer be counted as incense before you,
>   and the lifting up of my hands as the evening sacrifice!

Cruciform 2
Prayer

> We entreat thee, O Lord,
> That this evening may be holy, good, and peaceful,
> That your holy angels may lead us in paths of peace and goodwill,
> That we may be pardoned and forgiven for our sins and offenses,
> That there may be peace in your Church and in the whole world,
> That we may depart this life in your faith and fear, and not be condemned before the great judgment seat of Christ,
> That we may be bound together by your Holy Spirit in the communion of all your saints, entrusting one another and all our life to Christ.

Week
Isaiah 6:3

> Holy, holy, holy, is the Lord of Hosts;
>   the whole earth is full of his glory!

Cruciform 3
A Collect for the Presence of Christ

> Lord Jesus, stay with us, for evening is at hand and the day is past; be our companion in the way, kindle our hearts, and awaken hope, that we may know you as you are revealed in Scripture and the breaking of bread. Grant this for the sake of your love. Amen.

The Anglican Rosary

Week

Psalm 16:7

> I will bless the Lord who gives me counsel;
> my heart teaches me, night after night.

Cruciform 4

The General Thanksgiving

> Almighty God, Father of all mercies,
>   we your unworthy servants give you humble thanks
>   for all your goodness and loving-kindness
>   to us and to all whom you have made.
> We bless you for our creation, preservation,
>   and all the blessings of this life;
>   but above all for your immeasurable love
>   in the redemption of the world by our Lord Jesus Christ;
>   for the means of grace, and for the hope of glory.
> And, we pray, give us such an awareness of your mercies,
>   that with truly thankful hearts we may show forth your praise,
>   not only with our lips, but in our lives,
>   by giving up our selves to your service,
>   and by walking before you
>   in holiness and righteousness all our days;
> Through Jesus Christ our Lord,
>   to whom, with you and the Holy Spirit,
>   be honor and glory throughout all ages. Amen.

Week

Psalm 16:8

> I have set the Lord always before me;
> because he is at my right hand, I shall not be shaken.

CRUCIFORM 1

The Lord's Prayer

> Our Father, who art in heaven,
>   hallowed be thy Name,
>   thy kingdom come,
>   thy will be done,
>   on earth as it is in heaven.
> Give us this day our daily bread.
> And forgive us our trespasses,
>   as we forgive those
>   who trespass against us.
> And lead us not into temptation,
>   but deliver us from evil.
> For thine is the kingdom,
>   and the power, and the glory,
>   for ever and ever. Amen.

INVITATORY

2 Corinthians 13:14

> The grace of our Lord Jesus Christ, and the love of God, and the fellowship of the Holy Spirit, be with us all evermore. Amen.

CROSS

> Glory be to the Father, and to the Son, and to the Holy Spirit; as it was in the beginning, is now, and ever shall be, world without end. Amen.

Compline I

Cross
In the name of the Father, the Son, and the Holy Spirit. Amen.

Invitatory
The Lord Almighty grant us a peaceful night and a perfect end.

Cruciform 1
Psalm 4:1-8

> Hear me when I call, O God of my righteousness;
>   you set me free when I was in trouble;
>   have mercy upon me, and hear my prayer.
> O you children of men, how long will you blaspheme my honor
>   And have such pleasure in vanity, and seek after falsehood?
> Know this also, that the Lord has chosen for himself
>   the one that is godly;
>   when I call upon the Lord, he will hear me.
> Stand in awe, and sin not;
>   commune with your own heart upon your bed, and be still.
> Offer the sacrifice of righteousness
>   and put your trust in the Lord.
> There are many who say, "Who will show us any good?"
>   Lord, lift up the light of your countenance upon us.
> You have put gladness in my heart,
>   more than when others' grain and wine and oil increased.
> I will lay myself down in peace, and take my rest;
>   for you, Lord, only, make me dwell in safety.

Week
Psalm 124:8

> Our help is in the Name of the Lord;
>   the maker of heaven and earth.

Cruciform 2
Matthew 11:28 30

> Come to me, all who labor and are heavy laden, and I will give you rest. Take my yoke upon you, and learn from me, for I am gentle and lowly in heart, and you will find rest for your souls. For my yoke is easy, and my burden is light.

Week

> O God, make speed to save us. O Lord, make haste to help us.

Cruciform 3

> Visit this place, O Lord, and drive far from it all snares of the enemy; let your holy angels dwell with us to preserve us in peace; and let your blessing be upon us always; through Jesus Christ our Lord. Amen.

Week

> Be our light in the darkness and preserve us in peace;
> let your blessing be upon us always.

Cruciform 4
Luke 2:29-32 Song of Simeon

> Lord, now let your servant depart in peace,
>   according to your word.
> For my eyes have seen your salvation,
>   which you have prepared before the face of all people;
> To be a light to lighten the Gentiles,
>   and to be the glory of your people Israel.
> Glory be to the Father, and to the Son, and to the Holy Spirit;
>   as it was in the beginning, is now, and ever shall be, world without end. Amen.

Week

> Guide us waking, O Lord, and guard us sleeping; that awake we may watch with Christ, and asleep we may rest in peace.

The Anglican Rosary

CRUCIFORM 1
The Lord's Prayer

Our Father, who art in heaven,
   hallowed be thy Name,
   thy kingdom come,
   thy will be done,
     on earth as it is in heaven.
Give us this day our daily bread.
And forgive us our trespasses,
   as we forgive those
     who trespass against us.
And lead us not into temptation,
   but deliver us from evil.
For thine is the kingdom,
   and the power, and the glory,
   for ever and ever. Amen.

INVITATORY

Keep watch, dear Lord, with those who work, or watch, or weep this night, and give your angels charge over those who sleep. Tend the sick, Lord Christ; give rest to the weary, bless the dying, soothe the suffering, pity the afflicted, shield the joyous; and all for your love's sake. Amen.

CROSS

The almighty and merciful Lord, Father, Son, and Holy Spirit, bless us and keep us, this night and evermore. Amen.

Morning Prayer II

Cross
Habakkuk 2:20

> The Lord is in his holy temple;
> let all the earth keep silence before him.

Invitatory
Jubilate   Be Joyful   Psalm 100

> O be joyful in the Lord, all you lands;
> serve the Lord with gladness, and come before
> his presence with a song.
> Be assured that the Lord he is God;
> it is he who has made us, and not we ourselves;
> we are his people, and the sheep of his pasture.
> O go your way into his gates with thanksgiving,
> and into his courts with praise;
> be thankful unto him, and speak good of his Name.
> For the Lord is gracious, his mercy is everlasting,
> and his truth endures from generation to generation.

Cruciform 1
Magna et mirabilia   The Song of the Redeemed   Revelation 15:3-4

> O ruler of the universe, Lord God,
> great deeds are they that you have done,
> surpassing human understanding.
> Your ways are ways of righteousness and truth,
> O King of all the ages.
> Who can fail to do you homage, Lord,
> and sing the praises of your Name?
> for you only are the Holy One.
> All nations will draw near and fall down before you,
> because your just and holy works have been revealed.

Week

> O Lord, reveal your just and holy works among the nations.

CRUCIFORM 2
Prayer

> O Lord, show your mercy upon us;
> and grant us your salvation.
> O Lord, guide those who govern us;
> and lead us in the way of justice and truth.
> Clothe your ministers with righteousness;
> and let your people sing with joy.
> O Lord, save your people;
> and bless your inheritance.
> Give peace in our time, O Lord;
> and defend us by your mighty power.
> Let not the needy, O Lord, be forgotten;
> nor the hope of the poor be taken away.
> Create in us clean hearts, O God;
> and take not your Holy Spirit from us.

WEEK

> Oh Lord, save your people; and bless your inheritance today.

CRUCIFORM 3
Collect for Peace

> O God, the author of peace and lover of concord, to know you is eternal life and to serve you is perfect freedom: Defend us, your humble servants, in all assaults of our enemies; that we, surely trusting in your defense, may not fear the power of any adversaries; through the might of Jesus Christ our Lord. Amen.

WEEK

> The mercy of the Lord is everlasting: O come, let us adore him.

CRUCIFORM 4
The General Thanksgiving

> Almighty God, Father of all mercies,
> we your unworthy servants give you humble thanks
> for all your goodness and loving-kindness
> to us and to all whom you have made.

Morning Prayer II

We bless you for our creation, preservation,
  and all the blessings of this life;
  but above all for your immeasurable love
  in the redemption of the world by our Lord Jesus Christ;
  for the means of grace, and for the hope of glory.
And, we pray, give us such an awareness of your mercies,
  that with truly thankful hearts we may show forth your praise,
  not only with our lips, but in our lives,
  by giving up our selves to your service,
  and by walking before you
  in holiness and righteousness all our days;
Through Jesus Christ our Lord,
  to whom, with you and the Holy Spirit,
  be honor and glory throughout all ages. Amen.

Week

The Lord is full of compassion and mercy:
O come, let us adore him.

Cruciform 1

The Lord's Prayer

Our Father, who art in heaven,
  hallowed be thy Name,
  thy kingdom come,
  thy will be done,
    on earth as it is in heaven.
Give us this day our daily bread.
And forgive us our trespasses,
  as we forgive those
    who trespass against us.
And lead us not into temptation,
  but deliver us from evil.
For thine is the kingdom,
  and the power, and the glory,
  for ever and ever. Amen.

Invitatory

2 Corinthians 13:14

> The grace of our Lord Jesus Christ, and the love of God, and the fellowship of the Holy Spirit, be with us all evermore. Amen.

Cross

> Glory be to the Father, and to the Son, and to the Holy Spirit; as it was in the beginning, is now, and ever shall be, world without end. Amen.

Midday Prayer II

Cross
In the name of the Father, the Son, and the Holy Spirit. Amen.

Invitatory
O God, make speed to save us.
O Lord, make haste to help us.

Cruciform 1
Psalm 121:1-4

I will lift up my eyes unto the hills;
   from whence comes my help?
My help comes from the Lord,
   who has made heaven and earth.
He will not let your foot be moved
   and he who keeps you will not sleep.
Behold, he who keeps Israel
   shall neither slumber nor sleep;

Week
Psalm 121:2

My help comes from the Lord,
   who has made heaven and earth.

Cruciform 2
2 Corinthians 5:17-18

If anyone is in Christ, he is a new creation. The old has passed away; behold, the new has come. All this is from God, who through Christ reconciled us to himself and gave us the ministry of reconciliation.

Week
Psalm 51:10

Create in me a clean heart, O God,
   and renew a right spirit within me

CRUCIFORM 3
Psalm 121:5-8

> The LORD himself is your keeper;
>   the LORD is your defense upon your right hand,
> So that the sun shall not burn you by day,
>   neither the moon by night.
> The LORD shall preserve you from all evil;
>   indeed, it is he who shall keep your soul.
> The LORD shall preserve your going out and your coming in,
>   from this time forth for evermore.

WEEK

> Preserve us from all evil, O Lord,
> and watch over our loved ones today.

CRUCIFORM 4

> Grant us, O Lord, we pray, the spirit to think and do always those things that are right, that we, who can do no good thing apart from you, may by you be enabled to live according to your will; through Jesus Christ our Lord, who lives and reigns with you and the Holy Spirit, one God, for ever and ever.

WEEK

> Lord have mercy, Christ have mercy.

CRUCIFORM 1
The Lord's Prayer

> Our Father, who art in heaven,
>   hallowed be thy Name,
>   thy kingdom come,
>   thy will be done,
>   on earth as it is in heaven.
> Give us this day our daily bread.
> And forgive us our trespasses,
>   as we forgive those
>   who trespass against us.
> And lead us not into temptation,
>   but deliver us from evil.

For thine is the kingdom,
  and the power, and the glory,
  for ever and ever. Amen.

INVITATORY

Blessed Savior, at this hour you hung on the cross, stretching out your loving arms: Grant that all the peoples of the earth may look to you and be saved; for your tender mercies' sake. Amen.

CROSS

Glory be to the Father, and to the Son, and to the Holy Spirit; as it was in the beginning, is now, and ever shall be, world without end. Amen.

Evening Prayer II

CROSS
Psalm 26:8

> O Lord, I love the habitation of your house and the place where your glory dwells.

INVITATORY
Phos hilaron   O Gladsome Light

> O gladsome light,
> pure brightness of the everliving Father in heaven,
>   O Jesus Christ, holy and blessed!
> Now as we come to the setting of the sun,
> and our eyes behold the vesper light,
>   we sing your praises, O God: Father, Son, and Holy Spirit.
> You are worthy at all times to be praised by happy voices,
>   O Son of God, O Giver of Life,
>   and to be glorified through all the worlds.

CRUCIFORM 1
Magnificat   The Song of Mary   Luke 1:46-55

> My soul magnifies the Lord,
>   and my spirit rejoices in God my Savior.
> For he has regarded
>   the lowliness of his handmaiden.
> For behold, from now on,
>   all generations will call me blessed.
> For he that is mighty has magnified me,
>   and holy is his Name.
> And his mercy is on those who fear him,
>   throughout all generations.
> He has shown the strength of his arm;
>   he has scattered the proud in the imagination of their hearts.
> He has brought down the mighty from their thrones,
>   and has exalted the humble and meek.

He has filled the hungry with good things,
   and the rich he has sent empty away.
He, remembering his mercy, has helped his servant Israel,
   as he promised to our fathers, Abraham and his seed for ever.

Week
Psalm 141:2

Let my prayer be counted as incense before you,
   and the lifting up of my hands as the evening sacrifice!

Cruciform 2
Prayer

We entreat thee, O Lord,
That this evening may be holy, good, and peaceful,
That your holy angels may lead us in paths of peace and goodwill,
That we may be pardoned and forgiven for our sins and offenses,
That there may be peace in your Church and in the whole world,
That we may depart this life in your faith and fear, and not be condemned before the great judgment seat of Christ,
That we may be bound together by your Holy Spirit in the communion of all your saints, entrusting one another and all our life to Christ.

Week
1 Corinthians 15:57

Thanks be to God, who gives us the victory through
our Lord Jesus Christ.

Cruciform 3
A Collect for Aid against Perils

Lighten our darkness, we beseech you, O Lord; and by your great mercy defend us from all perils and dangers of this night; for the love of your only Son, our Savior Jesus Christ. Amen.

The Anglican Rosary

Week
Psalm 16:7-8

> I will bless the LORD who gives me counsel; my heart teaches me, night after night.

Cruciform 4
The General Thanksgiving

> Almighty God, Father of all mercies,
>   we your unworthy servants give you humble thanks
>   for all your goodness and loving-kindness
>   to us and to all whom you have made.
> We bless you for our creation, preservation,
>   and all the blessings of this life;
>   but above all for your immeasurable love
>   in the redemption of the world by our Lord Jesus Christ;
>   for the means of grace, and for the hope of glory.
> And, we pray, give us such an awareness of your mercies,
>   that with truly thankful hearts we may show forth your praise,
>   not only with our lips, but in our lives,
>   by giving up our selves to your service,
>   and by walking before you
>   in holiness and righteousness all our days;
> Through Jesus Christ our Lord,
>   to whom, with you and the Holy Spirit,
>   be honor and glory throughout all ages. Amen.

Week
Psalm 16:8

> I have set the LORD always before me;
>   because he is at my right hand, I shall not be shaken.

Cruciform 1
The Lord's Prayer

> Our Father, who art in heaven,
>   hallowed be thy Name,
>   thy kingdom come,
>   thy will be done,
>   on earth as it is in heaven.

Give us this day our daily bread.
And forgive us our trespasses,
  as we forgive those
    who trespass against us.
And lead us not into temptation,
  but deliver us from evil.
For thine is the kingdom,
  and the power, and the glory,
    for ever and ever. Amen.

INVITATORY

Romans 15:13

May the God of hope fill us with all joy and peace in believing through the power of the Holy Spirit. Amen.

CROSS

Glory be to the Father, and to the Son, and to the Holy Spirit; as it was in the beginning, is now, and ever shall be, world without end. Amen.

Compline II

Cross
In the name of the Father, the Son, and the Holy Spirit. Amen.

Invitatory
The Lord Almighty grant us a peaceful night and a perfect end.

Cruciform 1
Psalm 31:1-6

In you, O Lord, have I put my trust;
  let me never be put to confusion;
  deliver me in your righteousness.
Bow down your ear to me;
  make haste to deliver me.
And be my strong rock, and house of defense,
  that you may save me.
For you are my strong rock and my castle;
  be also my guide, and lead me for your Name's sake.
Draw me out of the net that they have laid secretly for me,
  for you are my strength.
Into your hands I commend my spirit,
  for you have redeemed me, O Lord, O God of truth.

Week
Our help is in the Name of the Lord;
the maker of heaven and earth.

Cruciform 2
Hebrews 13:20-21

Now may the God of peace who brought again from the dead our Lord Jesus, the great shepherd of the sheep, by the blood of the eternal covenant, equip you with everything good that you may do his will, working in us that which is pleasing in his sight, through Jesus Christ, to whom be glory forever and ever.

Week

O God, make speed to save us. O Lord, make haste to help us.

Cruciform 3

Lighten our darkness, we beseech you, O Lord; and by your great mercy defend us from all perils and dangers of this night; for the love of your only Son, our Savior Jesus Christ. Amen.

Week

Be our light in the darkness and preserve us in peace;
let your blessing be upon us always.

Cruciform 4

Luke 2:29-32 Song of Simeon

Lord, now let your servant depart in peace,
 according to your word.
For my eyes have seen your salvation,
 which you have prepared before the face of all people;
To be a light to lighten the Gentiles,
 and to be the glory of your people Israel.
Glory be to the Father, and to the Son, and to the Holy Spirit;
 as it was in the beginning, is now, and ever shall be, world without end. Amen.

Week

Guide us waking, O Lord, and guard us sleeping; that awake we may watch with Christ, and asleep we may rest in peace.

Cruciform 1

The Lord's Prayer

Our Father, who art in heaven,
 hallowed be thy Name,
 thy kingdom come,
 thy will be done,
  on earth as it is in heaven.

Give us this day our daily bread.
And forgive us our trespasses,
　as we forgive those
　　who trespass against us.
And lead us not into temptation,
　but deliver us from evil.
For thine is the kingdom,
　and the power, and the glory,
　for ever and ever. Amen.

Invitatory

O God, your unfailing providence sustains the world we live in and the life we live: Watch over those, both night and day, who work while others sleep, and grant that we may never forget that our common life depends upon each other's toil; through Jesus Christ our Lord. Amen.

Cross

The almighty and merciful Lord, Father, Son, and Holy Spirit, bless us and keep us, this night and evermore. Amen.

Morning Prayer III

CROSS

Philippians 1:2

> Grace to you and peace from God our Father and the Lord Jesus Christ.

INVITATORY

Surge, illuminare   Arise, shine, for your light has come
Isaiah 60:1-3, 11a, 14c, 18-19

> Arise, shine, for your light has come,
>   and the glory of the Lord has dawned upon you.
> For behold, darkness covers the land;
>   deep gloom enshrouds the peoples.
> But over you the Lord will rise,
>   and his glory will appear upon you.
> Nations will stream to your light,
>   and kings to the brightness of your dawning.
> Your gates will always be open;
>   by day or night they will never be shut.
> They will call you, The City of the Lord,
>   the Zion of the Holy One of Israel.
> Violence will no more be heard in your land,
>   ruin or destruction within your borders.
> You will call your walls, Salvation,
>   and all your portals, Praise.
> The sun will no more be your light by day;
>   by night you will not need the brightness of the moon.
> The Lord will be your everlasting light,
>   and your God will be your glory.

CRUCIFORM 1

Benedictus   The Song of Zechariah   Luke 1:68-79

> Blessed be the Lord, the God of Israel;
>   he has come to his people and set them free.
> He has raised up for us a mighty savior,
>   born of the house of his servant David.

Through his holy prophets he promised of old,
> that he would save us from our enemies,
> from the hands of all who hate us.

He promised to show mercy to our fathers
> and to remember his holy covenant.

This was the oath he swore to our father Abraham,
> to set us free from the hands of our enemies,

Free to worship him without fear,
> holy and righteous in his sight
> all the days of our life.

You, my child, shall be called the prophet of the Most High,
> for you will go before the Lord to prepare his way,

To give his people knowledge of salvation
> by the forgiveness of their sins.

In the tender compassion of our God
> the dawn from on high shall break upon us,

To shine on those who dwell in darkness
> and in the shadow of death,
> and to guide our feet into the way of peace.

WEEK

Lord, shine on those who dwell in darkness
and guide our feet into the way of peace.

CRUCIFORM 2

Prayer

> O Lord, show your mercy upon us;
>> and grant us your salvation.
>
> O Lord, guide those who govern us;
>> and lead us in the way of justice and truth.
>
> Clothe your ministers with righteousness;
>> and let your people sing with joy.
>
> O Lord, save your people;
>> and bless your inheritance.
>
> Give peace in our time, O Lord;
>> and defend us by your mighty power.
>
> Let not the needy, O Lord, be forgotten;
>> nor the hope of the poor be taken away.
>
> Create in us clean hearts, O God;
>> and take not your Holy Spirit from us.

Week

Give peace in our time, O Lord;
and defend us by your mighty power.

Cruciform 3
A Collect for Grace

O Lord, our heavenly Father, almighty and everlasting God, you have brought us safely to the beginning of this day: Defend us by your mighty power, that we may not fall into sin nor run into any danger; and that guided by your Spirit, we may do what is righteous in your sight; through Jesus Christ our Lord. Amen.

Week

The mercy of the Lord is everlasting: O come, let us adore him.

Cruciform 4
The General Thanksgiving

Almighty God, Father of all mercies,
   we your unworthy servants give you humble thanks
   for all your goodness and loving-kindness
   to us and to all whom you have made.
We bless you for our creation, preservation,
   and all the blessings of this life;
   but above all for your immeasurable love
   in the redemption of the world by our Lord Jesus Christ;
   for the means of grace, and for the hope of glory.
And, we pray, give us such an awareness of your mercies,
   that with truly thankful hearts we may show forth your praise,
   not only with our lips, but in our lives,
   by giving up our selves to your service,
   and by walking before you
   in holiness and righteousness all our days;
Through Jesus Christ our Lord,
   to whom, with you and the Holy Spirit,
   be honor and glory throughout all ages. Amen.

The Anglican Rosary

Week

Christ the Lord has ascended into heaven:
O come, let us adore him.

Cruciform 1
The Lord's Prayer

Our Father, who art in heaven,
   hallowed be thy Name,
   thy kingdom come,
   thy will be done,
     on earth as it is in heaven.
Give us this day our daily bread.
And forgive us our trespasses,
   as we forgive those
     who trespass against us.
And lead us not into temptation,
   but deliver us from evil.
For thine is the kingdom,
   and the power, and the glory,
   for ever and ever. Amen.

Invitatory
Ephesians 3:20-21

Glory to God whose power, working in us, can do infinitely more than we can ask or imagine: Glory to him from generation to generation in the Church, and in Christ Jesus for ever and ever. Amen.

Cross

Glory be to the Father, and to the Son, and to the Holy Spirit; as it was in the beginning, is now, and ever shall be, world without end. Amen.

Midday Prayer III

CROSS
In the name of the Father, the Son, and the Holy Spirit. Amen.

INVITATORY
O God, make speed to save us.
O Lord, make haste to help us.

CRUCIFORM 1
Psalm 124:1-3

If the LORD himself had not been on our side,
   now may Israel say;
if the LORD had not been on our side,
   when men rose up against us;
Then would they have swallowed us up alive
   when they were so wrathfully displeased with us;
Then the waters would have drowned us,
   and the torrent gone over us;
Then the raging waters would have gone clean over us.

WEEK
The Lord himself is on our side, let us adore him.

CRUCIFORM 2
John 12:31-32

Jesus said, "Now is the judgment of this world; now will the ruler of this world be cast out. And I, when I am lifted up from the earth, will draw all people to myself."

WEEK
2 Corinthians 13:14

The grace of our Lord Jesus Christ, and the love of God, and the fellowship of the Holy Spirit, be with us all evermore.

Cruciform 3
Psalm 124:4-6

> But praised be the Lord
> who has not given us over to be a prey for their teeth.
> We have escaped even as a bird out of the snare of the fowler;
> the snare is broken, and we have been delivered.
> Our help is in the Name of the Lord,
> the maker of heaven and earth.

Week

> Our help is in the Name of the Lord, the maker of heaven and earth.

Cruciform 4

> O Lord God, grant your people grace to withstand the temptations of the world, the flesh, and the devil, and with pure hearts and minds to follow you, the only God; through Jesus Christ our Lord, who lives and reigns with you and the Holy Spirit, one God, now and for ever.

Week 4

> Lord have mercy, Christ have mercy.

Cruciform 1
The Lord's Prayer

> Our Father, who art in heaven,
> hallowed be thy Name,
> thy kingdom come,
> thy will be done,
> on earth as it is in heaven.
> Give us this day our daily bread.
> And forgive us our trespasses,
> as we forgive those
> who trespass against us.
> And lead us not into temptation,
> but deliver us from evil.
> For thine is the kingdom,
> and the power, and the glory,
> for ever and ever. Amen.

Midday Prayer III

INVITATORY

Father of all mercies, you revealed your boundless compassion to your apostle Saint Peter in a three-fold vision: Forgive our unbelief, we pray, and so strengthen our hearts and enkindle our zeal, that we may fervently desire the salvation of all people, and diligently labor in the extension of your kingdom; through him who gave himself for the life of the world, your Son our Savior Jesus Christ.

CROSS

Glory be to the Father, and to the Son, and to the Holy Spirit; as it was in the beginning, is now, and ever shall be, world without end. Amen.

Evening Prayer III

Cross
Psalm 141:2

> Let my prayer be set forth in your sight as incense,
>> the lifting up of my hands as the evening sacrifice.

Invitatory
Phos hilaron   O Gladsome Light

> O gladsome light,
> pure brightness of the everliving Father in heaven,
>> O Jesus Christ, holy and blessed!
> Now as we come to the setting of the sun,
> and our eyes behold the vesper light,
>> we sing your praises, O God: Father, Son, and Holy Spirit.
> You are worthy at all times to be praised by happy voices,
>> O Son of God, O Giver of Life,
>> and to be glorified through all the worlds.

Cruciform 1
Ecce, Deus   Surely, it is God who saves me   Isaiah 12:2-6

> Surely, it is God who saves me;
>> I will trust in him and not be afraid.
> For the Lord is my stronghold and my sure defense,
>> and he will be my Savior.
> Therefore you shall draw water with rejoicing
>> from the springs of salvation.
> And on that day you shall say,
>> Give thanks to the Lord and call upon his Name;
> Make his deeds known among the peoples;
>> see that they remember that his Name is exalted.
> Sing the praises of the Lord, for he has done great things,
>> and this is known in all the world.
> Cry aloud, inhabitants of Zion, ring out your joy,
>> for the great one in the midst of you is the Holy One of Israel.

Evening Prayer III

Week
Isaiah 12:2

> Surely, it is God who saves me;
> I will trust in him and not be afraid.

Cruciform 2
Prayer

> We entreat thee, O Lord,
> That this evening may be holy, good, and peaceful,
> That your holy angels may lead us in paths of peace and goodwill,
> That we may be pardoned and forgiven for our sins and offenses,
> That there may be peace in your Church and in the whole world,
> That we may depart this life in your faith and fear, and not be condemned before the great judgment seat of Christ,
> That we may be bound together by your Holy Spirit in the communion of all your saints, entrusting one another and all our life to Christ.

Week
Isaiah 60:3

> Nations shall come to your light,
> and kings to the brightness of your rising.

Cruciform 3
A Collect for Faith

> Lord Jesus Christ, by your death you took away the sting of death: Grant to us your servants so to follow in faith where you have led the way, that we may at length fall asleep peacefully in you and wake up in your likeness; for your tender mercies' sake. Amen.

Week
Psalm 16:7-8

> I will bless the LORD who gives me counsel;
> my heart teaches me, night after night.

Cruciform 4
The General Thanksgiving

    Almighty God, Father of all mercies,
        we your unworthy servants give you humble thanks
        for all your goodness and loving-kindness
        to us and to all whom you have made.
    We bless you for our creation, preservation,
        and all the blessings of this life;
        but above all for your immeasurable love
        in the redemption of the world by our Lord Jesus Christ;
        for the means of grace, and for the hope of glory.
    And, we pray, give us such an awareness of your mercies,
        that with truly thankful hearts we may show forth your praise,
        not only with our lips, but in our lives,
        by giving up our selves to your service,
        and by walking before you
        in holiness and righteousness all our days;
    Through Jesus Christ our Lord,
        to whom, with you and the Holy Spirit,
        be honor and glory throughout all ages. Amen.

Week
Psalm 16:8

    I have set the Lord always before me;
        because he is at my right hand, I shall not be shaken.

Cruciform 1
The Lord's Prayer

    Our Father, who art in heaven,
        hallowed be thy Name,
        thy kingdom come,
        thy will be done,
             on earth as it is in heaven.
    Give us this day our daily bread.
    And forgive us our trespasses,
        as we forgive those
            who trespass against us.

And lead us not into temptation,
   but deliver us from evil.
For thine is the kingdom,
   and the power, and the glory,
   for ever and ever. Amen.

INVITATORY

2 Corinthians 13:14

The grace of our Lord Jesus Christ, and the love of God, and the fellowship of the Holy Spirit, be with us all evermore. Amen.

CROSS

Glory be to the Father, and to the Son, and to the Holy Spirit; as it was in the beginning, is now, and ever shall be, world without end. Amen.

Compline III

Cross
In the name of the Father, the Son, and the Holy Spirit. Amen.

Invitatory
The Lord Almighty grant us a peaceful night and a perfect end.

Cruciform 1
Psalm 91:1-16

> Whoever dwells under the defense of the Most High
> > shall abide under the shadow of the Almighty.
>
> I will say unto the Lord,
> > "You are my refuge and my stronghold,
> > my God in whom I will trust."
>
> For he shall deliver you from the snare of the hunter
> > and from the deadly pestilence.
>
> He shall defend you under his wings,
> > and you shall be safe under his feathers;
> > his faithfulness and truth shall be your shield and buckler.
>
> You shall not be afraid of any terror by night,
> > nor of the arrow that flies by day;
>
> Of the pestilence that walks in the darkness,
> > nor of the sickness that destroys at noonday.
>
> A thousand shall fall beside you,
> > and ten thousand at your right hand,
> > but it shall not come near you.
>
> Indeed, with your eyes you shall behold
> > and see the reward of the ungodly.
>
> For you, Lord, are my refuge;
> > you have set your house of defense very high.
>
> There shall no evil happen unto you,
> > neither shall any plague come near your dwelling.
>
> For he shall give his angels charge over you,
> > to keep you in all your ways.
>
> They shall bear you in their hands,
> > that you not hurt your foot against a stone.

You shall tread upon the lion and adder;
   the young lion and the serpent you shall trample under your feet.
Because he has set his love upon me, therefore I will deliver him;
   I have set him up, because he has known my Name.
He shall call upon me, and I will hear him;
   indeed, I am with him in trouble;
   I will deliver him and bring him to honor.
With long life I will satisfy him,
   and show him my salvation.

Week

Our help is in the Name of the LORD;
the maker of heaven and earth.

Cruciform 2

Jeremiah 14:9

You, O LORD, are in the midst of us, and we are called by your Name: do not forsake us.

Week

O God, make speed to save us. O Lord, make haste to help us.

Cruciform 3

Be present, O merciful God, and protect us through the hours of this night, so that we who are wearied by the changes and chances of this life may rest in your eternal changelessness; through Jesus Christ our Lord. Amen.

Week

Be our light in the darkness and preserve us in peace;
let your blessing be upon us always.

Cruciform 4

Luke 2:29-32 Song of Simeon

Lord, now let your servant depart in peace,
   according to your word.
For my eyes have seen your salvation,
   which you have prepared before the face of all people;

To be a light to lighten the Gentiles,
  and to be the glory of your people Israel.
Glory be to the Father, and to the Son, and to the Holy Spirit;
  as it was in the beginning, is now, and ever shall be, world without end. Amen.

Week

Guide us waking, O Lord, and guard us sleeping; that awake we may watch with Christ, and asleep we may rest in peace.

Cruciform 1

The Lord's Prayer

Our Father, who art in heaven,
  hallowed be thy Name,
  thy kingdom come,
  thy will be done,
    on earth as it is in heaven.
Give us this day our daily bread.
And forgive us our trespasses,
  as we forgive those
    who trespass against us.
And lead us not into temptation,
  but deliver us from evil.
For thine is the kingdom,
  and the power, and the glory,
  for ever and ever. Amen.

Invitatory

Keep watch, dear Lord, with those who work, or watch, or weep this night, and give your angels charge over those who sleep. Tend the sick, Lord Christ; give rest to the weary, bless the dying, soothe the suffering, pity the afflicted, shield the joyous; and all for your love's sake. Amen.

Cross

The almighty and merciful Lord, Father, Son, and Holy Spirit, bless us and keep us, this night and evermore. Amen.

Morning Prayer IV

CROSS

Psalm 122:1

> I was glad when they said to me,
> "Let us go to the house of the Lord!"

INVITATORY

Cantemus Domino   The Song of Moses   Exodus 15:1-6, 11-13, 17-18

> I will sing to the Lord, for he is lofty and uplifted;
>   the horse and its rider has he hurled into the sea.
> The Lord is my strength and my refuge;
>   the Lord has become my Savior.
> This is my God and I will praise him,
>   the God of my people and I will exalt him.
> The Lord is a mighty warrior;
>   The Lord is his Name.
> The chariots of Pharaoh and his army has he hurled into the sea;
>   the finest of those who bear armor have been drowned
>   in the Red Sea.
> The fathomless deep has overwhelmed them;
>   they sank into the depths like a stone.
> Your right hand, O Lord, is glorious in might;
>   your right hand, O Lord, has overthrown the enemy.
> Who can be compared with you, O Lord, among the gods?
>   who is like you, glorious in holiness,
>   awesome in renown, and worker of wonders?
> You stretched forth your right hand;
>   the earth swallowed them up.
> With your constant love you led the people you redeemed;
>   you brought them in safety to your holy dwelling.
> You will bring them in and plant them
>   on the mount of your possession,
> The resting-place you have made for yourself, O Lord,
>   the sanctuary, O Lord, that your hand has established.
> The Lord shall reign
>   for ever and for ever.

CRUCIFORM 1

Quaerite Dominum   Seek the Lord while he wills to be found   Isaiah 55:6-11

Seek the Lord while he wills to be found;
  call upon him when he draws near.
Let the wicked forsake their ways
  and the evil ones their thoughts;
And let them turn to the Lord, and he will have compassion,
  and to our God, for he will richly pardon.
For my thoughts are not your thoughts,
  nor your ways my ways, says the Lord.
For as the heavens are higher than the earth,
  so are my ways higher than your ways,
  and my thoughts than your thoughts.
For as rain and snow fall from the heavens
  and return not again, but water the earth,
Bringing forth life and giving growth,
  seed for sowing and bread for eating,
So is my word that goes forth from my mouth;
  it will not return to me empty;
But it will accomplish that which I have purposed,
  and prosper in that for which I sent it.

WEEK

Worship the Lord in the beauty of holiness:
O come let us adore him.

CRUCIFORM 2

Prayer

O Lord, show your mercy upon us;
  and grant us your salvation.
O Lord, guide those who govern us;
  and lead us in the way of justice and truth.
Clothe your ministers with righteousness;
  and let your people sing with joy.
O Lord, save your people;
  and bless your inheritance.
Give peace in our time, O Lord;
  and defend us by your mighty power.

Let not the needy, O Lord, be forgotten;
    nor the hope of the poor be taken away.
Create in us clean hearts, O God;
    and take not your Holy Spirit from us.

Week

O Lord, show your mercy upon us;
lead us in the way of justice and truth.

Cruciform 3
A Collect for the Renewal of Life

O God, the King eternal, whose light divides the day from the night and turns the shadow of death into the morning: Drive far from us all wrong desires, incline our hearts to keep your law, and guide our feet into the way of peace; that, having done your will with cheerfulness during the day, we may, when night comes, rejoice to give you thanks; through Jesus Christ our Lord. Amen.

Week

The mercy of the Lord is everlasting: O come, let us adore him.

Cruciform 4
The General Thanksgiving

Almighty God, Father of all mercies,
    we your unworthy servants give you humble thanks
    for all your goodness and loving-kindness
    to us and to all whom you have made.
We bless you for our creation, preservation,
    and all the blessings of this life;
    but above all for your immeasurable love
    in the redemption of the world by our Lord Jesus Christ;
    for the means of grace, and for the hope of glory.
And, we pray, give us such an awareness of your mercies,
    that with truly thankful hearts we may show forth your praise,
    not only with our lips, but in our lives,
    by giving up our selves to your service,
    and by walking before you
    in holiness and righteousness all our days;

Through Jesus Christ our Lord,
   to whom, with you and the Holy Spirit,
   be honor and glory throughout all ages. Amen.

Week

The Spirit of the Lord renews the face of the earth:
O come, let us adore him.

Cruciform 1

The Lord's Prayer

Our Father, who art in heaven,
   hallowed be thy Name,
   thy kingdom come,
   thy will be done,
      on earth as it is in heaven.
Give us this day our daily bread.
And forgive us our trespasses,
   as we forgive those
      who trespass against us.
And lead us not into temptation,
   but deliver us from evil.
For thine is the kingdom,
   and the power, and the glory,
   for ever and ever. Amen.

Invitatory

Colossians 3:1

If then you have been raised with Christ, seek the things that are above, where Christ is, seated at the right hand of God.

Cross

Glory be to the Father, and to the Son, and to the Holy Spirit; as it was in the beginning, is now, and ever shall be, world without end. Amen.

Midday Prayer IV

Cross
In the name of the Father, the Son, and the Holy Spirit. Amen.

Invitatory
O God, make speed to save us.
O Lord, make haste to help us.

Cruciform 1
Psalm 126:1-3

When the Lord overturned the captivity of Zion,
   then were we like those who dream.
Then was our mouth filled with laughter,
   and our tongue with shouts of joy.
Then they said among the nations,
   "The Lord has done great things for them."

Week
The Lord has done great things for us, come let us adore him.

Cruciform 2
Malachi 1:11

From the rising of the sun to its setting my Name will be great among the nations, and in every place incense will be offered to my Name, and a pure offering. For my Name will be great among the nations, says the Lord of Hosts.

Week
Holy and great is the Name of our God,
may all people and nations praise you.

Cruciform 3
Psalm 126:4-7

> Indeed, the LORD has done great things for us already,
> > Whereof we rejoice.
>
> Overturn our captivity, O LORD,
> > as the rivers in the south.
>
> Those who sow in tears
> > shall reap in joy.
>
> He who goes on his way weeping, and bears good seed,
> > shall doubtless come again with joy, and bring his sheaves with him.

Week

> The Lord has done great things for us, come let us adore him.

Cruciform 4

> Almighty and merciful God, it is only by your grace that your faithful people offer you true and laudable service: Grant that we may run without stumbling to obtain your heavenly promises; through Jesus Christ our Lord, who lives and reigns with you and the Holy Spirit, one God, now and for ever. Amen.

Week

> Lord have mercy, Christ have mercy.

Cruciform 1
The Lord's Prayer

> Our Father, who art in heaven,
> > hallowed be thy Name,
> > thy kingdom come,
> > thy will be done,
> > > on earth as it is in heaven.
>
> Give us this day our daily bread.
> And forgive us our trespasses,
> > as we forgive those
> > > who trespass against us.
>
> And lead us not into temptation,
> > but deliver us from evil.

For thine is the kingdom,
  and the power, and the glory,
  for ever and ever. Amen.

INVITATORY

Pour your grace into our hearts, O Lord, that we who have known the incarnation of your Son Jesus Christ, announced by an angel to the Virgin Mary, may by his cross and passion be brought to the glory of his resurrection; who lives and reigns with you, in the unity of the Holy Spirit, one God, now and for ever.

CROSS

Glory be to the Father, and to the Son, and to the Holy Spirit; as it was in the beginning, is now, and ever shall be, world without end. Amen.

Evening Prayer IV

Cross

Psalm 16:7-8

> I will bless the Lord who gives me counsel; my heart teaches me, night after night. I have set the Lord always before me; because he is at my right hand, I shall not fall.

Invitatory

Phos hilaron   O Gladsome Light

> O gladsome light,
> pure brightness of the everliving Father in heaven,
>> O Jesus Christ, holy and blessed!
> Now as we come to the setting of the sun,
> and our eyes behold the vesper light,
>> we sing your praises, O God: Father, Son, and Holy Spirit.
> You are worthy at all times to be praised by happy voices,
>> O Son of God, O Giver of Life,
>> and to be glorified through all the worlds.

Cruciform 1

Deus misereatur   God be merciful   Psalm 67

> God be merciful unto us, and bless us,
>> and show us the light of his countenance, and be merciful unto us:
> That your way may be known upon earth,
>> your saving health among all nations.
> Let the peoples praise you, O God;
>> indeed, let all the peoples praise you.
> Oh, let the nations rejoice and be glad,
>> for you shall judge the people righteously,
>> and govern the nations upon earth.
> Let the peoples praise you, O God;
>> let all the peoples praise you.
> Then shall the earth bring forth her increase,
>> and God, even our own God, shall give us his blessing.
> God shall bless us,
>> and all the ends of the world shall fear him.

Week

Psalm 141:2

> Let my prayer be counted as incense before you,
> and the lifting up of my hands as the evening sacrifice!

Cruciform 2

Prayer

> We entreat thee, O Lord,
> That this evening may be holy, good, and peaceful,
> That your holy angels may lead us in paths of peace and goodwill,
> That we may be pardoned and forgiven for our sins and offenses,
> That there may be peace in your Church and in the whole world,
> That we may depart this life in your faith and fear, and not be condemned before the great judgment seat of Christ,
> That we may be bound together by your Holy Spirit in the communion of all your saints, entrusting one another and all our life to Christ.

Week

Psalm 96:9

> Worship the LORD in the beauty of holiness;
> let the whole earth tremble before him.

Cruciform 3

A Collect for Protection

> O God, the life of all who live, the light of the faithful, the strength of those who labor, and the repose of the dead: We thank you for the blessings of the day that is past, and humbly ask for your protection through the coming night. Bring us in safety to the morning hours; through him who died and rose again for us, your Son our Savior Jesus Christ. Amen.

Week

Psalm 16:7-8

> I will bless the LORD who gives me counsel;
> my heart teaches me, night after night.

CRUCIFORM 4
The General Thanksgiving

> Almighty God, Father of all mercies,
> > we your unworthy servants give you humble thanks
> > for all your goodness and loving-kindness
> > to us and to all whom you have made.
>
> We bless you for our creation, preservation,
> > and all the blessings of this life;
> > but above all for your immeasurable love
> > in the redemption of the world by our Lord Jesus Christ;
> > for the means of grace, and for the hope of glory.
>
> And, we pray, give us such an awareness of your mercies,
> > that with truly thankful hearts we may show forth your praise,
> > not only with our lips, but in our lives,
> > by giving up our selves to your service,
> > and by walking before you
> > in holiness and righteousness all our days;
>
> Through Jesus Christ our Lord,
> > to whom, with you and the Holy Spirit,
> > be honor and glory throughout all ages. Amen.

WEEK
Psalm 16:8

> I have set the LORD always before me;
> > because he is at my right hand, I shall not be shaken.

CRUCIFORM 1
The Lord's Prayer

> Our Father, who art in heaven,
> > hallowed be thy Name,
> > thy kingdom come,
> > thy will be done,
> > > on earth as it is in heaven.
>
> Give us this day our daily bread.
> And forgive us our trespasses,
> > as we forgive those
> > > who trespass against us.

And lead us not into temptation,
>   but deliver us from evil.
> For thine is the kingdom,
>   and the power, and the glory,
>   for ever and ever. Amen.

INVITATORY

Ephesians 3:20-21

Glory to God whose power, working in us, can do infinitely more than we can ask or imagine: Glory to him from generation to generation in the Church, and in Christ Jesus for ever and ever. Amen.

CROSS

Glory be to the Father, and to the Son, and to the Holy Spirit; as it was in the beginning, is now, and ever shall be, world without end. Amen.

Compline IV

Cross
In the name of the Father, the Son, and the Holy Spirit. Amen.

Invitatory
The Lord Almighty grant us a peaceful night and a perfect end.

Cruciform 1
Psalm 134:1-4

Behold now, praise the Lord,
 all you servants of the Lord.
You that stand by night in the house of the Lord,
 even in the courts of the house of our God.
Lift up your hands in the sanctuary
 and sing praises unto the Lord.
The Lord who made heaven and earth
 give you blessing out of Zion.

Week
Our help is in the Name of the Lord;
the maker of heaven and earth.

Cruciform 2
1 Peter 5:8 9a

Be sober-minded, be watchful. Your adversary the devil prowls around like a roaring lion, seeking someone to devour. Resist him, firm in your faith.

Week
O God, make speed to save us. O Lord, make haste to help us.

Cruciform 3

Look down, O Lord, from your heavenly throne, illumine this night with your celestial brightness, and from the children of light banish the deeds of darkness; through Jesus Christ our Lord. Amen.

Week

Be our light in the darkness and preserve us in peace;
let your blessing be upon us always.

Cruciform 4

Luke 2:29-32   Song of Simeon

Lord, now let your servant depart in peace,
   according to your word.
For my eyes have seen your salvation,
   which you have prepared before the face of all people;
To be a light to lighten the Gentiles,
   and to be the glory of your people Israel.
Glory be to the Father, and to the Son, and to the Holy Spirit;
   as it was in the beginning, is now, and ever shall be, world without end. Amen.

Week

Guide us waking, O Lord, and guard us sleeping; that awake we may watch with Christ, and asleep we may rest in peace.

Cruciform 1

The Lord's Prayer

Our Father, who art in heaven,
   hallowed be thy Name,
   thy kingdom come,
   thy will be done,
      on earth as it is in heaven.
Give us this day our daily bread.
And forgive us our trespasses,
   as we forgive those
      who trespass against us.

And lead us not into temptation,
   but deliver us from evil.
For thine is the kingdom,
   and the power, and the glory,
   for ever and ever. Amen.

INVITATORY

O God, your unfailing providence sustains the world we live in and the life we live: Watch over those, both night and day, who work while others sleep, and grant that we may never forget that our common life depends upon each other's toil; through Jesus Christ our Lord. Amen.

CROSS

The almighty and merciful Lord, Father, Son, and Holy Spirit, bless us and keep us, this night and evermore. Amen.

~4~

Holy Mysteries

God is the one who satisfies the passion for justice, the longing for spirituality, the hunger for relationship, the yearning for beauty. And God, the true God, is the God we see in Jesus of Nazareth, Israel's Messiah, the world's true Lord.
—N.T. Wright, Simply Christian: Why Christianity Makes Sense

As an Anglican, I embrace both Catholic and Protestant traditions. So, with encouragement from friends at a nearby convent, I set about learning how to pray the Catholic Rosary and the Holy Mysteries. As I delved into the events of Jesus' life, passion, and resurrection on a regular basis, it drew me closer to him.

The Holy Mysteries are groups of Scripture portraying the key events in Jesus' life. The Joyful Mysteries cover his conception, birth and early childhood. The Sorrowful Mysteries portray the passion of Christ beginning in the garden and ending with his crucifixion. The Glorious/Luminous Mysteries celebrate the spiritual ascendancy of Christ through his baptism, ascension, transfiguration, and resurrection.

Meditating on the key events of Jesus' life transforms our understanding of who he is. Our relationship with him becomes tangible and alive. I found such peace, comfort, and help, praying this way I wanted to share the experience with my non-Catholic friends, so I adapted the Mysteries for use with the Anglican Rosary.

Jesus is the heart of Christianity. The key events in his life compose the back story of our faith. Contemplating on these Mysteries enables us to fully comprehend God's love through the sacrifice and redemption of his Son. The Holy Mysteries reveal the heart of Christ as we enter into the light of his life, suffering, and glory.

While the Catholic Rosary relies on Mary as a guide for meditation on Jesus' life, the Anglican Rosary uses the Jesus Prayer[2] and Holy Scripture as aids for contemplation. For those who embrace Mary, I highly recommend using a Catholic Rosary. For others who respect, but do not revere Mary, I offer here an alternative for prayer and meditation on the life of Christ.

How to Pray this Rosary

The Cruciform heading for each Mystery states the name of the event in Jesus' life, the focus, or fruit of our meditation on it, and the scripture reference.

There are several ways to approach this Rosary. Different personalities will find one method more profitable than others. Though initially it's beneficial to use the method you relate to most, I encourage you to periodically use other styles as well. Sometimes getting out of our comfort zone allows God to reveal himself to us in new ways.

INTUITIVELY:
To pray through the mysteries intuitively the reader must remain open to the leading and prompting of the Holy Spirit. Focus on your heart as you read the Scripture out loud. Be sensitive to any words or phrases that jump out, or pictures or memories that come to mind. Whatever you see or hear during the reading will be what you meditate on as you recite the Week beads.

SENSING:
The mysteries come alive in the present when read through our senses. As you read the Scriptures, imagine you are there. Who are you in this setting? Where are you? What do you see? How are you feeling? What is God saying to you in this moment? Meditate on your experience as you move through the Week beads that follow.

---

[2] See page 129 for more on the Jesus Prayer

THINKING:

Although the idea of using a Rosary is to get out of our heads and into our hearts, it doesn't mean we abandon our thoughts. To contemplate requires thinking. When you approach the mysteries thoughtfully, you keep your heart open as you ponder what God is doing. What is the purpose of this mystery? What has it accomplished? How does this affect your life today? These and other questions that arise from reading thoughtfully will guide you to what the Holy Spirit wants to reveal in your life.

Joyful Mysteries

Cross

The Lord's Prayer

Our Father, who art in heaven,
  hallowed be thy Name,
  thy kingdom come,
  thy will be done,
    on earth as it is in heaven.
Give us this day our daily bread.
And forgive us our trespasses,
  as we forgive those
    who trespass against us.
And lead us not into temptation,
  but deliver us from evil.
For thine is the kingdom,
  and the power, and the glory,
  for ever and ever. Amen.

Invitatory

The Annunciation: Humility — Luke 1:26-28, 30-31, 35, 38

In the sixth month the angel Gabriel was sent from God to a city of Galilee named Nazareth, to a virgin betrothed to a man whose name was Joseph, of the house of David. And the virgin's name was Mary. And he came to her and said, "Greetings, O favored one, the Lord is with you!"

And the angel said to her, "Do not be afraid, Mary, for you have found favor with God. And behold, you will conceive in your womb and bear a son, and you shall call his name Jesus.

And the angel answered her, "The Holy Spirit will come upon you, and the power of the Most High will overshadow you; therefore the child to be borne will be called holy—the Son of God.

And Mary said, "Behold, I am the servant of the Lord; let it be to me according to your word." And the angel departed from her.

Pray: In the unexpected changes of life, may I humbly accept with a sincere heart and surrendered will all that you allow in my life.

Joyful Mysteries

CRUCIFORM 1
The Visitation: Charity — Luke 1:39-42, 45

In those days Mary arose and went with haste into the hill country, to a town in Judah, and she entered the house of Zechariah and greeted Elizabeth. And when Elizabeth heard the greeting of Mary, the baby leaped in her womb. And Elizabeth was filled with the Holy Spirit, and she exclaimed with a loud cry, "Blessed are you among women, and blessed is the fruit of your womb!

And blessed is she who believed that there would be a fulfillment of what was spoken to her from the Lord."

WEEK
Meditate on charity and love of neighbor.

Lord Jesus Christ, Son of God, have mercy on me, a sinner.

CRUCIFORM 2
The Birth of Our Lord: Poverty, or detachment from the world — Luke 2:7-14

And she gave birth to her firstborn son and wrapped him in swaddling cloths and laid him in a manger, because there was no place for them in the inn.

And in the same region there were shepherds out in the field, keeping watch over their flock by night. And an angel of the Lord appeared to them, and the glory of the Lord shone around them, and they were filled with great fear. And the angel said to them, "Fear not, for behold, I bring you good news of great joy that will be for all the people. For unto you is born this day in the city of David a Savior, who is Christ the Lord. And this will be a sign for you: you will find a baby wrapped in swaddling cloths and lying in a manger." And suddenly there was with the angel a multitude of the heavenly host praising God and saying,

"Glory to God in the highest,
and on earth peace among those with whom he is pleased!"

WEEK
Meditate on compassion for the poor, and deliverance from greed, sin, and envy.

Lord Jesus Christ, Son of God, have mercy on me, a sinner.

CRUCIFORM 3
The Presentation of Our Lord: Obedience — Luke 2:22-30

And when the time came for their purification according to the Law of Moses, they brought him up to Jerusalem to present him to the Lord (as it is written in the Law of the Lord, "Every male who first opens the womb shall be called holy to the Lord") and to offer a sacrifice according to what is said in the Law of the Lord, "a pair of turtledoves, or two young pigeons."

Now there was a man in Jerusalem, whose name was Simeon, and this man was righteous and devout, waiting for the consolation of Israel, and the Holy Spirit was upon him. And it had been revealed to him by the Holy Spirit that he would not see death before he had seen the Lord's Christ. And he came in the Spirit into the temple, and when the parents brought in the child Jesus, to do for him according to the custom of the Law, he took him up in his arms and blessed God and said,

"Lord, now you are letting your servant depart in peace,
 according to your word; for my eyes have seen your salvation."

WEEK
Meditate on obedience and fulfilling all that is right and good in God's eyes.

Lord Jesus Christ, Son of God, have mercy on me, a sinner.

CRUCIFORM 4
The finding of Our Lord in the Temple: Piety — Luke 2:41-49; 52

Now his parents went to Jerusalem every year at the Feast of the Passover. And when he was twelve years old, they went up according to custom. And when the feast was ended, as they were returning, the boy Jesus stayed behind in Jerusalem. His parents did not know it, but supposing him to be in the group they went a day's journey, but then they began to search for him among their relatives and acquaintances, and when they did not find him, they returned to Jerusalem, searching for him.

After three days they found him in the temple, sitting among the teachers, listening to them and asking them questions. And all who heard him were amazed at his understanding and his answers. And when his parents saw him, they were astonished. And his mother said to him, "Son, why have you treated us so? Behold, your father and I have been searching for you in great distress."

And he said to them, "Why were you looking for me? Did you not know that I must be in my Father's house?"

And Jesus increased in wisdom and in stature and in favor with God and man.

Week

Meditate on the importance of choosing God's way instead of the world's.

Lord Jesus Christ, Son of God, have mercy on me, a sinner.

Cruciform 1

Glory be to the Father, and to the Son, and to the Holy Spirit; as it was in the beginning, is now, and ever shall be, world without end. Amen.

Invitatory

Prayer of Our Lady of Fatima

O my Jesus, forgive us our sins, save us from the fires of hell. Lead all souls to heaven, especially those in most need of thy mercy.

Cross

Heavenly Father, your Son's life, death, and resurrection has purchased for us the rewards of eternal life; grant us grace while meditating on these sacred mysteries that we may imitate what they contain, and obtain what they promise. Through Christ our Lord, Amen.

Sorrowful Mysteries

CROSS

The Lord's Prayer

> Our Father, who art in heaven,
>   hallowed be thy Name,
>   thy kingdom come,
>   thy will be done,
>   on earth as it is in heaven.
> Give us this day our daily bread.
> And forgive us our trespasses,
>   as we forgive those
>   who trespass against us.
> And lead us not into temptation,
>   but deliver us from evil.
> For thine is the kingdom,
>   and the power, and the glory,
>   for ever and ever. Amen.

INVITATORY

The Agony in the Garden: Sorrow for sin — Matthew 26:36-40

> Then Jesus went with them to a place called Gethsemane, and he said to his disciples, "Sit here, while I go over there and pray." And taking with him Peter and the two sons of Zebedee, he began to be sorrowful and troubled. Then he said to them, "My soul is very sorrowful, even to death; remain here, and watch with me." And going a little farther he fell on his face and prayed, saying, "My Father, if it be possible, let this cup pass from me; nevertheless, not as I will, but as you will." And he came to the disciples and found them sleeping. And he said to Peter, "So, could you not watch with me one hour?"

> **Pray:** You suffered all for me, dear Jesus, that I might be saved. Grant me true contrition for sin. I desire to spend as much time with you as possible. In your presence, I find strength and courage to face the world.

Sorrowful Mysteries

Cruciform 1

The Scourging at the Pillar: Purity — Mark 15:12-15, Galations 2:20

And Pilate again said to them, "Then what shall I do with the man you call the King of the Jews?" And they cried out again, "Crucify him." And Pilate said to them, "Why? What evil has he done?" But they shouted all the more, "Crucify him." So Pilate, wishing to satisfy the crowd, released for them Barabbas, and having scourged Jesus, he delivered him to be crucified.

I have been crucified with Christ. It is no longer I who live, but Christ who lives in me. And the life I now live in the flesh I live by faith in the Son of God, who loved me and gave himself for me.

Week

Meditate on having a pure heart before God.

Lord Jesus Christ, Son of God, have mercy on me, a sinner.

Cruciform 2

The Crowning with Thorns: Courage — Mark 15:16-20, Isaiah 53:3-7

And the soldiers led him away inside the palace (that is, the governor's headquarters), and they called together the whole battalion. And they clothed him in a purple cloak, and twisting together a crown of thorns, they put it on him. And they began to salute him, "Hail, King of the Jews!" And they were striking his head with a reed and spitting on him and kneeling down in homage to him. And when they had mocked him, they stripped him of the purple cloak and put his own clothes on him. And they led him out to crucify him.

He was despised and rejected by men,
  a man of sorrows and acquainted with grief;
and as one from whom men hide their faces
  he was despised, and we esteemed him not.
    Surely he has borne our griefs
      and carried our sorrows;
    yet we esteemed him stricken,
      smitten by God, and afflicted.
    But he was pierced for our transgressions;
      he was crushed for our iniquities;

upon him was the chastisement that brought us peace,
   and with his wounds we are healed.
All we like sheep have gone astray;
   we have turned—every one—to his own way;
and the LORD has laid on him
   the iniquity of us all.

WEEK

Meditate on moral courage in the face of opposition.

Lord Jesus Christ, Son of God, have mercy on me, a sinner.

CRUCIFORM 3

The Carrying of the Cross: Patience — John 19:16-17, Luke 23:26-28

So they took Jesus, and he went out, bearing his own cross, to the place called The Place of a Skull, which in Aramaic is called Golgotha.

And as they led him away, they seized one Simon of Cyrene, who was coming in from the country, and laid on him the cross, to carry it behind Jesus. And there followed him a great multitude of the people and of women who were mourning and lamenting for him. But turning to them Jesus said, "Daughters of Jerusalem, do not weep for me, but weep for yourselves and for your children.

WEEK

Meditate on patience in the midst of hardship and caring for others.

Lord Jesus Christ, Son of God, have mercy on me, a sinner.

CRUCIFORM 4

The Crucifixion: Perseverance — John 19:28-30, Philippians 2:1-8

After this, Jesus, knowing that all was now finished, said (to fulfill the Scripture), "I thirst." A jar full of sour wine stood there, so they put a sponge full of the sour wine on a hyssop branch and held it to his mouth. When Jesus had received the sour wine, he said, "It is finished," and he bowed his head and gave up his spirit.

So if there is any encouragement in Christ, any comfort from love, any participation in the Spirit, any affection and sympathy, complete my joy by being of the same mind, having the same love, being in full accord and of one mind. Do nothing from selfish ambition or conceit, but in humility count others more significant than yourselves. Let each of you look not only to his own interests, but also to the interests of others. Have this mind among yourselves, which is yours in Christ Jesus, who, though he was in the form of God, did not count equality with God a thing to be grasped, but emptied himself, by taking the form of a servant, being born in the likeness of men. And being found in human form, he humbled himself by becoming obedient to the point of death, even death on a cross.

WEEK

Meditate on perseverance and surrender to God's will.

Lord Jesus Christ, Son of God, have mercy on me, a sinner.

CRUCIFORM 1

Glory be to the Father, and to the Son, and to the Holy Spirit; as it was in the beginning, is now, and ever shall be, world without end. Amen.

INVITATORY

Prayer of Our Lady of Fatima

O my Jesus, forgive us our sins, save us from the fires of hell. Lead all souls to heaven, especially those in most need of thy mercy.

CROSS

Heavenly Father, your Son's life, death, and resurrection has purchased for us the rewards of eternal life; grant us grace while meditating on these sacred mysteries that we may imitate what they contain, and obtain what they promise. Through Christ our Lord, Amen.

Glorious/Luminous Mysteries

Cross

The Lord's Prayer

> Our Father, who art in heaven,
> hallowed be thy Name,
> thy kingdom come,
> thy will be done,
> on earth as it is in heaven.
> Give us this day our daily bread.
> And forgive us our trespasses,
> as we forgive those
> who trespass against us.
> And lead us not into temptation,
> but deliver us from evil.
> For thine is the kingdom,
> and the power, and the glory,
> for ever and ever. Amen.

Invitatory

Baptism of Jesus: Openness to the Holy Spirit — Matthew 3:13, 16-17

> Then Jesus came from Galilee to the Jordan to John, to be baptized by him. . . . And when Jesus was baptized, immediately he went up from the water, and behold, the heavens were opened to him, and he saw the Spirit of God descending like a dove and coming to rest on him; and behold, a voice from heaven said, "This is my beloved Son, with whom I am well pleased."

> **Pray:** God of grace and glory, You call us with Your voice of flame to be your people, faithful and courageous. As Your beloved Son embraced his mission in the waters of baptism, inspire us with the fire of your Spirit to join in his transforming work.[3]

---

3 Revised Common Lectionary Prayers

Cruciform 1

The Transfiguration: Desire for Holiness — Luke 9:28-32, 34-36

Now about eight days after these sayings he took with him Peter and John and James and went up on the mountain to pray. And as he was praying, the appearance of his face was altered, and his clothing became dazzling white. And behold, two men were talking with him, Moses and Elijah, who appeared in glory and spoke of his departure, which he was about to accomplish at Jerusalem. Now Peter and those who were with him were heavy with sleep, but when they became fully awake they saw his glory and the two men who stood with him. . . . A cloud came and overshadowed them, and they were afraid as they entered the cloud. And a voice came out of the cloud, saying, "This is my Son, my Chosen One; listen to him!" And when the voice had spoken, Jesus was found alone. And they kept silent and told no one in those days anything of what they had seen.

Week

Meditate on the desire to be a new person in Christ.

Lord Jesus Christ, Son of God, have mercy on me, a sinner.

Cruciform 2

The Resurrection: Faith — Matthew 28:5-10, 1 Corinthians 15:3-4

The angel said to the women, "Do not be afraid, for I know that you seek Jesus who was crucified. He is not here, for he has risen, as he said. Come, see the place where he lay. Then go quickly and tell his disciples that he has risen from the dead, and behold, he is going before you to Galilee; there you will see him. See, I have told you." So they departed quickly from the tomb with fear and great joy, and ran to tell his disciples. And behold, Jesus met them and said, "Greetings!" And they came up and took hold of his feet and worshiped him. Then Jesus said to them, "Do not be afraid; go and tell my brothers to go to Galilee, and there they will see me."

For I delivered to you as of first importance what I also received: that Christ died for our sins . . . that he was buried, that he was raised on the third day in accordance with the Scriptures.

Week

Meditate on the strength of your faith and sharing it with others.

Lord Jesus Christ, Son of God, have mercy on me, a sinner.

Cruciform 3

The Ascension: Hope — Acts 1:6-8, Luke 24:50-52

So when they had come together, they asked him, "Lord, will you at this time restore the kingdom to Israel?" He said to them, "It is not for you to know times or seasons that the Father has fixed by his own authority. But you will receive power when the Holy Spirit has come upon you, and you will be my witnesses in Jerusalem and in all Judea and Samaria, and to the end of the earth."

And he led them out as far as Bethany, and lifting up his hands he blessed them. While he blessed them, he parted from them and was carried up into heaven. And they worshiped him and returned to Jerusalem with great joy, and were continually in the temple blessing God.

Week

Meditate on the joy of hope found in Christ.

Lord Jesus Christ, Son of God, have mercy on me, a sinner.

Cruciform 4

The Gift of the Holy Spirit: Love of God — John 16:7-11, Acts 2:1-4

Nevertheless, I tell you the truth: it is to your advantage that I go away, for if I do not go away, the Helper will not come to you. But if I go, I will send him to you. And when he comes, he will convict the world concerning sin and righteousness and judgment: concerning sin, because they do not believe in me; concerning righteousness, because I go to the Father, and you will see me no longer; concerning judgment, because the ruler of this world is judged.

When the day of Pentecost arrived, they were all together in one place. And suddenly there came from heaven a sound like a mighty rushing wind, and it filled the entire house where they were sitting. And divided tongues as of fire appeared to them and rested on each one of them. And they were all filled with the Holy Spirit and began to speak in other tongues as the Spirit gave them utterance.

WEEK

Meditate on the love of God manifested through the Holy Spirit's presence with us.

Lord Jesus Christ, Son of God, have mercy on me, a sinner.

CRUCIFORM 1

Glory be to the Father, and to the Son, and to the Holy Spirit; as it was in the beginning, is now, and ever shall be, world without end. Amen.

INVITATORY

Prayer of Our Lady of Fatima

O my Jesus, forgive us our sins, save us from the fires of hell. Lead all souls to heaven, especially those in most need of thy mercy.

CROSS

Heavenly Father, your Son's life, death, and resurrection has purchased for us the rewards of eternal life; grant us grace while meditating on these sacred mysteries that we may imitate what they contain, and obtain what they promise. Through Christ our Lord, Amen.

~5~
A.C.T.S. Prayer

More things are wrought by prayer than this world dreams of.
—*Alfred Lord Tennyson*

When people talk about praying they usually mean asking for something. Whether it's for healing, provision, or help, we are supposed to ask God to supply our needs. Unfortunately, we get so caught up in asking, we forget prayer is also a dialogue. It is the means through which God has a relationship with us, as well as how he works in our lives. The transformational power of prayer comes when we connect with God in such a way that we are receiving even as we ask.

Prayer has always been a vital and active part of the church. Through prayer, the apostles were transformed from fearful men into courageous witnesses for Christ. They were nourished, strengthened, and encouraged by God's life-giving presence to meet the challenges they faced each day.

Our prayers are life-changing when we focus more on God than on our troubles. He is the source of life and offers the peace that passes understanding. Scripture reminds us it's through praise and thanksgiving that we connect with God. As we bare our souls in the midst of his unconditional love, we receive encouragement and blessing. The lies of the world are exposed, and we find our true identity in him.

A helpful guide for praying in this manner is to use the acronym A.C.T.S. which stands for:

Adoration
Confession
Thanksgiving
Supplication

A.C.T.S.

The A.C.T.S. prayer model has been used by Christians everywhere since the 1800s. The Rosary easily combines these four steps of praying with the beads to allow time to delve deeply into our relationship with God. Those who pray this way open the storehouse of his riches, which are vital for personal growth and wholeness.

Let's look at the significance of each step.

ADORATION means to love greatly and worship as divine. It is the act of praising and honoring God with your whole heart. Adoring God raises your spirit to the heavenly realm where troubles melt like ice before the warmth of the sun. The more you engage in this discipline of worship the more time you will want to spend in adoration.

CONFESSION acknowledges our shortcomings before God. It's good to search our hearts in humility and with honesty before the One who offers forgiveness. Admitting our own sin makes it easier to forgive others. It frees us to move forward in relationships and to be renewed in our spirits. Confession also prepares us to receive the gifts God wants to bestow on us.

THANKSGIVING recognizes all that's good in our lives comes from God. Here we reflect on how we've been blessed and acknowledge God for his protection and provision in our lives. We show gratitude for all he's done already and for what he's going to do in the future. We thank God for the strength and comfort of the Holy Spirit.and for always being with us, especially in difficult times.

SUPPLICATION is the process of humbly requesting or petitioning God for our needs. Now that our perspective is aligned with who God is, and how he's already provided, we can set our concerns before him with faith, knowing in our hearts he will answer.

This order makes all the difference in prayer. By the time we get to what we are asking for, we already have the assurance God is listening and will act on our behalf.

The Anglican Rosary

How to Pray this Rosary

The instructions for praying each section of the A.C.T.S. prayer are included in the Rosary on the following page. It's important to have a willingness to enter into each step of prayer without expectations or judgment. The Holy Spirit will guide your prayer time. Relax and enjoy each step as you enter into communion with God.

The Cruciform beads have Scriptures to prepare your heart for each act of worship. Recite them with enthusiasm and confidence. The Week beads then provide an opportunity to listen as you pray. Each section has a prompt, or cue, to get you started (I pray for…, I thank you for…, etc.).

Don't plan ahead or think about what you are going to pray—simply begin the sentence and allow what bubbles to the surface to be expressed. Pray whatever comes to your mind first. Follow in this manner by repeating the prompt and praying the next inspiration on each of the Week beads.

It's easy to get stuck in the should of and ought to of how we pray. The A.C.T.S model asks you to trust the Holy Spirit to bring what is important to your attention. The more you relax and not worry about the process, the easier it becomes to be spontaneous. This is a very gratifying way to pray because you give the responsibility for your prayer time to God.

A.C.T.S Rosary

Cross
In the name of the Father, the Son, and the Holy Spirit. Amen.

Invitatory
Psalm 25:8-10

> Good and upright is the Lord;
>   therefore he instructs sinners in the way.
> He leads the humble in what is right,
>   and teaches the humble his way.
> All the paths of the Lord are steadfast love and faithfulness,
>   for those who keep his covenant and his testimonies.

Cruciform 1 - ADORATION
Psalm 103:1-5

> Bless the Lord, O my soul,
>   and all that is within me,
>   bless his holy name!
> Bless the Lord, O my soul,
>   and forget not all his benefits,
> who forgives all your iniquity,
>   who heals all your diseases,
> who redeems your life from the pit,
>   who crowns you with steadfast love and mercy,
> who satisfies you with good
>   so that your youth is renewed like the eagle's.

Week
Worship God for who he is. Bless his holy name as Healer, Provider, Creator of heaven and earth, the Lord our God, Father who Forgives, Sanctifier, God Most High, God who Sees, Abba Father.

> Bless the Lord, O my soul, and all that is within me.
> I bless your holy name, for you…

Cruciform 2 – CONFESSION
Hosea 14:1-7, Psalm 103:8-13

>Return, O Israel, to the Lord your God,
>>for you have stumbled because of your iniquity.
>
>Take with you words
>>and return to the Lord;
>
>say to him,
>>"Take away all iniquity;
>
>accept what is good,
>>and we will pay with bulls
>>the vows of our lips.
>
>Assyria shall not save us;
>>we will not ride on horses;
>
>and we will say no more, 'Our God,'
>>to the work of our hands.
>
>In you the orphan finds mercy."
>
>The Lord is merciful and gracious,
>>slow to anger and abounding in steadfast love.
>
>He will not always chide,
>>nor will he keep his anger forever.
>
>He does not deal with us according to our sins,
>>nor repay us according to our iniquities.
>
>For as high as the heavens are above the earth,
>>so great is his steadfast love toward those who fear him;
>
>as far as the east is from the west,
>>so far does he remove our transgressions from us.
>
>As a father shows compassion to his children,
>>so the Lord shows compassion to those who fear him.

Week

Ask for God's forgiveness. Confess your sins and acknowledge where you've fallen short loving and caring for others. As you come before God with a repentant heart, forgive those who've hurt you, and forgive yourself. Your Father in heaven accepts and loves you even when you fall and fail to do what's right.

>O Lord, forgive me for…

Cruciform 3 – THANKSGIVING
1 Chronicles 16:8-13, 34

> Oh give thanks to the Lord; call upon his name;
> > make known his deeds among the peoples!
> Sing to him, sing praises to him;
> > tell of all his wondrous works!
> Glory in his holy name;
> > let the hearts of those who seek the Lord rejoice!
> Seek the Lord and his strength;
> > seek his presence continually!
> Remember the wondrous works that he has done,
> > his miracles and the judgments he uttered,
> O offspring of Israel his servant,
> > children of Jacob, his chosen ones!
> Oh give thanks to the Lord, for he is good;
> > for his steadfast love endures forever!

Week

Use the following phrase on each bead and thank God for his care and concern, and for all that is good in your life.

> Lord, you are good, your love endures forever.
> Thank you for…

Cruciform 4 – SUPPLICATION
Psalm 86:6-10 (NASB)

> Give ear, O Lord, to my prayer;
> > And give heed to the voice of my supplications!
> In the day of my trouble I shall call upon You,
> > For You will answer me.
> There is no one like You among the gods, O Lord,
> > Nor are there any works like Yours.
> All nations whom You have made shall come and worship before You, O Lord,
> > And they shall glorify Your name.
> For You are great and do wondrous deeds;
> > You alone are God.

The Anglican Rosary

Week

Pour out the desires of your heart before the One who hears and will answer. Ask for healing, provision, help, and peace. Release all frustrations about the past and fears for the future, knowing as you give your heart and your loved ones to the Lord—he will provide.

O Lord, I pray for…

Cruciform 1
Psalm 28:6-9

> Blessed be the Lord!
>   For he has heard the voice of my pleas for mercy.
> The Lord is my strength and my shield;
>   in him my heart trusts, and I am helped;
>   my heart exults,
>   and with my song I give thanks to him.
> The Lord is the strength of his people;
>   he is the saving refuge of his anointed.
> Oh, save your people and bless your heritage!
>   Be their shepherd and carry them forever.

Invitatory
1 Chronicles 16:23-27

> Sing to the Lord, all the earth!
>   Tell of his salvation from day to day.
> Declare his glory among the nations,
>   his marvelous works among all the peoples!
> For great is the Lord, and greatly to be praised,
>   and he is to be feared above all gods.
> For all the gods of the peoples are worthless idols,
>   but the Lord made the heavens.
> Splendor and majesty are before him;
>   strength and joy are in his place.

Cross
Psalm 19:14

> Let the words of my mouth and the meditation of my heart
>   be acceptable in your sight,
>   O Lord, my rock and my redeemer.

~6~

Saint Patrick's Breastplate

*It was in the strength of God that I went –
God who turned the direction of my life to good.*
—St. Patrick

Ireland's beloved Saint Patrick penned a beautiful prayer of protection that is as relevant today as it was fifteen hundred years ago. Known as Saint Patrick's Breastplate, this lyrical prayer was turned into a mighty hymn of faith in the 1800s. It is sung each year in March to commemorate the Saint and his passion to convert pagans to Christianity.

The word breastplate has multiple references. As a piece of armor, the breastplate protects the heart in battle. In medieval times knights placed inscriptions of prayers into their armor which they recited as they rode into battle. Jewish priests were mandated to wear breastplates as part of their clothing in Exodus, reminding them of God's covenant and promises. In other parts of the Bible, breastplate is used symbolically to signify protection from unrighteousness.

Christian faith is a shield against evil. Saint Patrick used this prayer in preparation prior to confronting pagan strongholds. As we navigate the uncertainties of life, we too can find help, protection, and courage through praying this prayer with the Rosary.

Saint Patrick's Breastplate is founded on the doctrine of the Trinity. The verses build on the power of Christ's redemption; invoking help from angels, patriarch's, saints and martyrs. It calls upon strength from creation and seeks wisdom and safety through communion with God.

Today our armor is spiritual, not physical. Confessing belief in Christ and the Trinity gives us the courage to face daily trials. Whenever I feel weak or uncertain, I pray Saint Patrick's Breastplate. This prepares me to face whatever challenges are ahead knowing God is with me—his strength and might will see me through.

How to Pray this Rosary

This Rosary differs from others in the book because the repeated phrase is on the Cruciform beads. The Week beads contain declarations of faith with an individual phrase for each bead. Rather than meditating on the Week beads we invoke the covering of Christ by praying this beautiful prayer out loud with confidence and assurance.

Saint Patrick's Breastplate's bold declaration of faith sets the spiritual realm on notice. We belong to Christ and his victory is what we stand on today. We recite this in preparation to go out into the world to do the work God has given us to do in the strength of our faith and with help from the Holy Spirit.

St. Patrick's Breastplate Rosary

Cross

I bind unto myself today the strong Name of the Trinity,
by invocation of the same, the Three in One, and One in Three.
Of whom all nature hath creation, eternal Father, Spirit, Word:
praise to the Lord of my salvation, salvation is of Christ the Lord.

Invitatory

Christ be with me, Christ within me, Christ behind me, Christ before me, Christ beside me, Christ to win me, Christ to comfort and restore me. Christ beneath me, Christ above me, Christ in quiet, Christ in danger, Christ in hearts of all that love me, Christ in mouth of friend and stranger.

Cruciform 1

I bind unto myself today the strong Name of the Trinity,
by invocation of the same, the Three in One, and One in Three.

Week

1. I bind this day to me for ever; by power of faith, Christ's incarnation;
2. his baptism in Jordan river;
3. his death on cross for my salvation;
4. his bursting from the spiced tomb;
5. his riding up the heavenly way;
6. his coming at the day of doom;
7. I bind unto myself today.

Cruciform 2

I bind unto myself today the strong Name of the Trinity,
by invocation of the same, the Three in One, and One in Three.

Week

1. I bind unto myself today the powerful love of cherubim;
2. the sweet "Well done" in judgment hour;
3. the service of the seraphim;
4. confessors' faith, apostles' word,
5. the patriarchs' prayers, the prophets' scrolls;
6. all good deeds done unto the Lord,
7. and purity of virgin souls.

Cruciform 3

I bind unto myself today the strong Name of the Trinity,
by invocation of the same, the Three in One, and One in Three.

Week

1. I bind unto myself today the virtues of the starlit heaven,
2. the glorious sun's life-giving ray,
3. the whiteness of the moon at even,
4. the flashing of the lightning free,
5. the whirling wind's tempestuous shocks,
6. the stable earth, the deep salt sea,
7. around the old eternal rocks.

Cruciform 4

I bind unto myself today the strong Name of the Trinity,
by invocation of the same, the Three in One, and One in Three.

Week

1. I bind unto myself today the power of God to hold and lead,
2. his eye to watch, his might to stay,
3. his ear to hearken to my need;
4. the wisdom of my God to teach,
5. his hand to guide, his shield to ward;
6. the word of God to give me speech,
7. his heavenly host to be my guard.

St. Patrick's Breastplate

CRUCIFORM 1

Christ be with me, Christ within me, Christ behind me, Christ before me, Christ beside me, Christ to win me, Christ to comfort and restore me. Christ beneath me, Christ above me, Christ in quiet, Christ in danger, Christ in hearts of all that love me, Christ in mouth of friend and stranger.

INVITATORY

I bind unto myself today the strong Name of the Trinity,
by invocation of the same, the Three in One, and One in Three.
Of whom all nature hath creation, eternal Father, Spirit, Word:
praise to the Lord of my salvation, salvation is of Christ the Lord.[4]

CROSS

In the name of the Father, the Son, and the Holy Spirit. Amen.

---

[4] Words: attributed to St. Patrick (372-466); translated by Cecil Frances Alexander, 1889. Adapted for use with Anglican Prayer Beads by Laura Kelly Campbell. Formated by Jenny Lynn Estes.

~7~

The Way of the Cross

*Our Savior's passion raises men and women from the depths,
lifts them up from the earth, and sets them in the heights.*
—St. Maximus of Turin

Before followers of Jesus were known as Christians, they were first called "The Way." Their encounter with Christ caused them to think, act, and love in revolutionary ways. They approached life in a manner different from cultural norms. As Christianity spread, people were drawn to connect with their risen Lord by walking the path he took to crucifixion. This pilgrimage in Jerusalem became known as the Via Dolorosa, or, the Way of Sorrows. The devotion grew in popularity until the time of the Crusades when traveling to Jerusalem became too dangerous.

At this point, churches began erecting symbolic stations using paintings, illustrations, and sculptures to represent the key elements of Christ's passion, so the faithful could take their pilgrimages at home. Today, this devotion is known as The Way of the Cross, or Stations of the Cross, and has become a vibrant way to pray and meditate on Christ's sacrifice for us.

The Way of the Cross teaches us how to respond to the misery we encounter in this world. We learn from Christ's example how to endure, forgive, surrender, and accept help. Suffering can be transformed and redeemed if we walk our path as Jesus did. In the midst of heartache, insults, trials, and pain we find the strength and hope to endure because he shows us the way of grace in the midst of hardship.

HOW TO PRAY THIS ROSARY

The fourteen Scriptural stations of the cross have been split into three Rosaries. These can be prayed one at a time, or all at once. Each Rosary begins with the Lord's Prayer. Take this moment to settle your soul in God's presence, silently releasing all cares and concerns as you focus your mind on Jesus. Allow the Holy Spirit to instruct your heart as you enter into the passion of your Savior.

The stations invite us to embrace loneliness, pain, and betrayal with love and mercy for those who harm and hurt us. Picture yourself in Jesus' place as the events unfold. How does it feel? What's going through your mind? Where do you find hope? Consider the actions and reactions of those surrounding him and his response to them. Where are you with Jesus—in the crowd, by the fire, or at the foot of the cross? How do you respond in a crisis?

Jesus' unwavering trust in the will of God gave him strength to endure in the midst of hate and persecution without succumbing to fear or despair. Where do you need to trust God today?

The individual stations of the cross are found on the Cruciform beads, followed by a short prayer in response. Prayerfully read and enter into each event with an open mind. Then hold that event in your heart as you repeat the refrain on the Week beads:

"I adore you, O Christ, and I bless you.

By your holy cross, you have redeemed the world."

This phrase is traditionally used as the opening refrain for each station of the cross. In this Rosary we use it for meditation on the Week beads. It captures the essence of the passion and the basis for our transformation; because Jesus redeemed us, we are able to become like him. He not only shows us the way to trust God in difficult times, but gives us the courage and hope to endure when we surrender our lives to him.

May the Holy Spirit guide, instruct, and comfort you as you partake in the passion of Christ.

The Way of the Cross Rosary I

Cross
The Lord's Prayer

> Our Father, who art in heaven,
>   hallowed be thy Name,
>   thy kingdom come,
>   thy will be done,
>   on earth as it is in heaven.
> Give us this day our daily bread.
> And forgive us our trespasses,
>   as we forgive those
>   who trespass against us.
> And lead us not into temptation,
>   but deliver us from evil.
> For thine is the kingdom,
>   and the power, and the glory,
>   for ever and ever. Amen.

Invitatory
Isaiah 53:5

> But he was pierced for our transgressions;
>   he was crushed for our iniquities;
> upon him was the chastisement that brought us peace,
>   and with his wounds we are healed.

Cruciform 1
First Station   Jesus Prays in Gethsemane   Matthew 26:36-39

> Then Jesus went with them to a place called Gethsemane, and he said to his disciples, "Sit here, while I go over there and pray." And taking with him Peter and the two sons of Zebedee, he began to be sorrowful and troubled. Then he said to them, "My soul is very sorrowful, even to death; remain here, and watch with me." And going a little farther he fell on his face and prayed, saying, "My Father, if it be possible, let this cup pass from me; nevertheless, not as I will, but as you will."

Pray: O Lord, in the midst of troubled times, may I find peace in praying your will be done. I turn to you for strength when pain and sorrow confront me. As I walk the way of the cross, may I find in it the way of life and hope.

Week

I adore you, O Christ, and I bless you.
By your holy cross, you have redeemed the world.

Cruciform 2

Second Station   Jesus Betrayed by Judas and Arrested   Matthew 26:47-50

While he was still speaking, Judas came, one of the twelve, and with him a great crowd with swords and clubs, from the chief priests and the elders of the people. Now the betrayer had given them a sign, saying, "The one I will kiss is the man; seize him." And he came up to Jesus at once and said, "Greetings, Rabbi!" And he kissed him. Jesus said to him, "Friend, do what you came to do." Then they came up and laid hands on Jesus and seized him.

Pray: Heavenly Father, I trust in your protection and support. Help me remain calm in the midst of uncertainty and danger. You hold my future in your hands. I stand in faith knowing you work all things together for good when I submit my will to yours.

Week

I adore you, O Christ, and I bless you.
By your holy cross, you have redeemed the world.

Cruciform 3

Third Station   Jesus Condemned by the Sanhedrin   Matthew 26:59-66

Now the chief priests and the whole council were seeking false testimony against Jesus that they might put him to death, but they found none, though many false witnesses came forward. At last two came forward and said, "This man said, 'I am able to destroy the temple of God, and to rebuild it in three days.'" And the high priest stood up and said, "Have you no answer to make? What is it that these men testify against you?" But Jesus remained silent. And the high priest said to him, "I adjure you by the living God, tell us if you are the Christ, the Son of God." Jesus said to him, "You have said so. But I tell you, from now on you will see the Son of Man seated at the right hand of Power and coming on the clouds of heaven." Then the high priest tore his robes and said, "He has uttered blasphemy. What further witnesses do we need? You have now heard his blasphemy. What is your judgment?" They answered, "He deserves death."

Pray: Thank you, God, you are always with me. May I be fearless in the face of opposition, valuing my relationship with you over the opinions of others. With steadfast heart, let the words of my mouth speak truth into the darkness of the world.

Week

I adore you, O Christ, and I bless you.
By your holy cross, you have redeemed the world.

Cruciform 4
Fourth Station   Peter Denies Jesus   Matthew 26:69-75

Now Peter was sitting outside in the courtyard. And a servant girl came up to him and said, "You also were with Jesus the Galilean." But he denied it before them all, saying, "I do not know what you mean." And when he went out to the entrance, another servant girl saw him, and she said to the bystanders, "This man was with Jesus of Nazareth." And again he denied it with an oath: "I do not know the man." After a little while the bystanders came up and said to Peter, "Certainly you too are one of them, for your accent betrays you." Then he began to invoke a curse on himself and to swear, "I do not know the man." And immediately the rooster crowed. And Peter remembered the saying of Jesus, "Before the rooster crows, you will deny me three times." And he went out and wept bitterly.

Pray: Lord, you knew Peter's frailty and faults and yet you loved him. May I love and forgive the difficult people in my life. And when I stumble, be gracious to help me repent, for a penitent heart keeps me in right relationship with you.

Week

I adore you, O Christ, and I bless you.
By your holy cross, you have redeemed the world.

Cruciform 1

Fifth Station   Jesus Judged by Pilate   Mark 15:4-15

And Pilate again asked him, "Have you no answer to make? See how many charges they bring against you." But Jesus made no further answer, so that Pilate was amazed. Now at the feast he used to release for them one prisoner for whom they asked. And among the rebels in prison, who had committed murder in the insurrection, there was a man called Barabbas. And the crowd came up and began to ask Pilate to do as he usually did for them. And he answered them, saying, "Do you want me to release for you the King of the Jews?" For he perceived that it was out of envy that the chief priests had delivered him up. But the chief priests stirred up the crowd to have him release for them Barabbas instead. And Pilate again said to them, "Then what shall I do with the man you call the King of the Jews?" And they cried out again, "Crucify him." And Pilate said to them, "Why? What evil has he done?" But they shouted all the more, "Crucify him." So Pilate, wishing to satisfy the crowd, released for them Barabbas, and having scourged Jesus, he delivered him to be crucified.

Pray: O Lord, help me remain quiet when I am judged. You know the intentions of my heart, ultimately it is before you I stand or fall. And forgive me when I condemn people without cause. Let me remember to look at others through your eyes of mercy.

I adore you, O Christ, and I bless you.
By your holy cross, you have redeemed the world.

Invitatory

Ephesians 2:8-10

For by grace you have been saved through faith. And this is not your own doing; it is the gift of God, not a result of works, so that no one may boast. For we are his workmanship, created in Christ Jesus for good works, which God prepared beforehand, that we should walk in them.

Cross

Glory to the Father, and to the Son and to the Holy Spirit; as it was in the beginning, is now, and ever shall be, world without end. Amen.

The Way of the Cross Rosary II

CROSS
The Lord's Prayer

> Our Father, who art in heaven,
>   hallowed be thy Name,
>   thy kingdom come,
>   thy will be done,
>   on earth as it is in heaven.
> Give us this day our daily bread.
> And forgive us our trespasses,
>   as we forgive those
>   who trespass against us.
> And lead us not into temptation,
>   but deliver us from evil.
> For thine is the kingdom,
>   and the power, and the glory,
>   for ever and ever. Amen.

INVITATORY
1 Peter 3:14-15

> But even if you should suffer for righteousness' sake, you will be blessed. Have no fear of them, nor be troubled, but in your hearts honor Christ the Lord.

CRUCIFORM 1
Sixth Station   Jesus Scourged and Crowned with Thorns...Matthew 27:27-30

> Then the soldiers of the governor took Jesus into the governor's headquarters, and they gathered the whole battalion before him. And they stripped him and put a scarlet robe on him, and twisting together a crown of thorns, they put it on his head and put a reed in his right hand. And kneeling before him, they mocked him, saying, "Hail, King of the Jews!" And they spit on him and took the reed and struck him on the head.

Pray: O Lord, you did not fight back when they broke your flesh. Give me the ability to accept the sufferings of my body and spirit with grace. Though the world may break me, my confidence in you sustains me.

Week

I adore you, O Christ, and I bless you.
By your holy cross, you have redeemed the world.

Cruciform 2

Seventh Station   Jesus Bears the Cross   Matthew 27:31

And when they had mocked him, they stripped him of the robe and put his own clothes on him and led him away to crucify him.

Pray: Precious Lord, you willingly endured the agony of the cross for my redemption. Accepting your will in my life gives me the courage to rise above fear and walk the path before me with grace.

Week

I adore you, O Christ, and I bless you.
By your holy cross, you have redeemed the world.

Cruciform 3

Eighth Station   Simon Helps Jesus Carry the Cross   Luke 23:26

And as they led him away, they seized one Simon of Cyrene, who was coming in from the country, and laid on him the cross, to carry it behind Jesus.

Pray: O Lord, may I accept help as you did when I'm tempted to do everything on my own. Then let my love for you provide the patience and courage to offer service to others whom I find in need.

Week

I adore you, O Christ, and I bless you.
By your holy cross, you have redeemed the world.

Cruciform 4

Ninth Station   Jesus Meets the Women of Jerusalem   Luke 23:27-31

And there followed him a great multitude of the people and of women who were mourning and lamenting for him. But turning to them Jesus said, "Daughters of Jerusalem, do not weep for me, but weep for yourselves and for your children. For behold, the days are coming when they will say, 'Blessed are the barren and the wombs that never bore and the breasts that never nursed!' Then they will begin to say to the mountains, 'Fall on us,' and to the hills, 'Cover us.' For if they do these things when the wood is green, what will happen when it is dry?"

Pray: Lord, you thought of others in the midst of your suffering. Preserve me from worldly anxieties and fear of the future. With the help of your Holy Spirit, I choose to abide in your light and presence as I walk the way of my cross.

Week

I adore you, O Christ, and I bless you.
By your holy cross, you have redeemed the world.

Cruciform 1

Tenth Station   Jesus is Crucified.   Luke 23:33-34

And when they came to the place that is called The Skull, there they crucified him, and the criminals, one on his right and one on his left. And Jesus said, "Father, forgive them, for they know not what they do."

Pray: Lord Jesus, you were pierced for my sins. Give me the courage to live free from selfishness and greed. Heal the wounds caused by prejudice, distrust, and hatred. And forgive me my trespasses as I forgive those who trespass against me.

I adore you, O Christ, and I bless you.
By your holy cross, you have redeemed the world.

INVITATORY

Philippians 2:5-11

> Have this mind among yourselves, which is yours in Christ Jesus, who, though he was in the form of God, did not count equality with God a thing to be grasped, but emptied himself, by taking the form of a servant, being born in the likeness of men. And being found in human form, he humbled himself by becoming obedient to the point of death, even death on a cross. Therefore God has highly exalted him and bestowed on him the name that is above every name, so that at the name of Jesus every knee should bow, in heaven and on earth and under the earth, and every tongue confess that Jesus Christ is Lord, to the glory of God the Father.

CROSS

> Glory to the Father, and to the Son and to the Holy Spirit; as it was in the beginning, is now, and ever shall be, world without end. Amen.

The Way of the Cross Rosary III

Cross
The Lord's Prayer

> Our Father, who art in heaven,
>   hallowed be thy Name,
>   thy kingdom come,
>   thy will be done,
>   on earth as it is in heaven.
> Give us this day our daily bread.
> And forgive us our trespasses,
>   as we forgive those
>   who trespass against us.
> And lead us not into temptation,
>   but deliver us from evil.
> For thine is the kingdom,
>   and the power, and the glory,
>   for ever and ever. Amen.

Invitatory
Ephesians 2:4-7

> But God, being rich in mercy, because of the great love with which he loved us, even when we were dead in our trespasses, made us alive together with Christ—by grace you have been saved—and raised us up with him and seated us with him in the heavenly places in Christ Jesus, so that in the coming ages he might show the immeasurable riches of his grace in kindness toward us in Christ Jesus.

Cruciform 1
Eleventh Station Jesus Promises His Kingdom to the Good Thief Luke 23:39-43

> One of the criminals who were hanged railed at him, saying, "Are you not the Christ? Save yourself and us!" But the other rebuked him, saying, "Do you not fear God, since you are under the same sentence of condemnation? And we indeed justly, for we are receiving the due reward of our deeds; but this man has done nothing wrong." And he said, "Jesus, remember me when you come into your kingdom." And he said to him, "Truly, I say to you, today you will be with me in paradise."

Pray: Lord, I acknowledge my wretchedness and worthily lament. Create in me a new and contrite heart, that I might live honorably here on earth, and in the fullness of time, join with you in glory.

Week

I adore you, O Christ, and I bless you.
By your holy cross, you have redeemed the world.

Cruciform 2

Twelfth Station   Jesus Speaks to His Mother and the Disciple   John 19:25-27

But standing by the cross of Jesus were his mother and his mother's sister, Mary the wife of Clopas, and Mary Magdalene. When Jesus saw his mother and the disciple whom he loved standing nearby, he said to his mother, "Woman, behold, your son!" Then he said to the disciple, "Behold, your mother!" And from that hour the disciple took her to his own home.

Pray: Lord Jesus, your last act of mercy was to care for your family. Help me embody the fourth commandment as you did by honoring my father and mother. May I be mindful to care for all my relations, including my spiritual family, for in this way, I also honor you.

Week

I adore you, O Christ, and I bless you.
By your holy cross, you have redeemed the world.

Cruciform 3

Thirteenth Station   Jesus Dies on the Cross   Matthew 27:45-50

Now from the sixth hour there was darkness over all the land until the ninth hour. And about the ninth hour Jesus cried out with a loud voice, saying, "Eli, Eli, lema sabachthani?" that is, "My God, my God, why have you forsaken me?" And some of the bystanders, hearing it, said, "This man is calling Elijah." And one of them at once ran and took a sponge, filled it with sour wine, and put it on a reed and gave it to him to drink. But the others said, "Wait, let us see whether Elijah will come to save him." And Jesus cried out again with a loud voice and yielded up his spirit.

The Anglican Rosary

Pray: Jesus, the great suffering you endured with the burden of my sin caused you to cry out in loneliness and separation from God. When I feel separated from you, help me not bury my pain, but release it daily by crying out to you for mercy. May the deep lament of my heart lead to new life and purpose, that I might join in the joy and freedom your death and resurrection bought for me.

Week

I adore you, O Christ, and I bless you.
By your holy cross, you have redeemed the world.

Cruciform 4

Fourteenth Station   Jesus Laid in the Tomb   Matthew 27:57-60

When it was evening, there came a rich man from Arimathea, named Joseph, who also was a disciple of Jesus. He went to Pilate and asked for the body of Jesus. Then Pilate ordered it to be given to him. And Joseph took the body and wrapped it in a clean linen shroud and laid it in his own new tomb, which he had cut in the rock. And he rolled a great stone to the entrance of the tomb and went away.

Pray: Praise God, who has not abandoned us to the grave, nor let his Holy One see corruption. His love for us endures forever. We, who have been buried in the waters of baptism, will find our perfect rest in God's eternal and glorious kingdom through the death and resurrection of his Son.

Week

I adore you, O Christ, and I bless you.
By your holy cross, you have redeemed the world.

Cruciform 1

Fifteenth Station   Jesus Rises from the Dead   Mark 16:4-7

And looking up, they saw that the stone had been rolled back—it was very large. And entering the tomb, they saw a young man sitting on the right side, dressed in a white robe, and they were alarmed. And he said to them, "Do not be alarmed. You seek Jesus of Nazareth, who was crucified. He has risen; he is not here.

See the place where they laid him. But go, tell his disciples and Peter that he is going before you to Galilee. There you will see him, just as he told you."

Pray: Blessed be the God and Father of our Lord Jesus Christ! According to his great mercy, he has caused us to be born again to a living hope through the resurrection of Jesus Christ from the dead.[5]

I adore you, O Christ, and I bless you.
By your holy cross, you have redeemed the world.

INVITATORY

Prayer After the Way of the Cross[6]

Dear Jesus, you are the living Word of God. You are the seed of everlasting life, and you fell to the earth by your death. But you rose to glorious life on that first Easter Sunday. You have taught us that Christian living is actually a dying to this world, and that this life is but a prelude to the eternity-long Easter that awaits us in your heavenly kingdom. Grant that on the last day, when you come again in glory upon the clouds of heaven to judge the living and the dead, bearing your cross as the sign of your triumph over sin and death, I may be able to show you my cross and hear you say: "Come, you blessed of my Father, into the kingdom prepared for you from all eternity." Amen.

CROSS

Glory to the Father, and to the Son and to the Holy Spirit; as it was in the beginning, is now, and ever shall be, world without end. Amen.

---

5 1 Peter 1:3

6 Fulton J. Sheen, *The Way of the Cross*, p.63 paraphrased

~8~
Lectio Divina

Lectio Divina is an opportunity to slow down and experience God's Word deeply. An opportunity to savor the words of Scripture, to sit at God's table to be nourished, fed and refreshed. An invitation to be fully present with our holy God.
—Cindee Snider Re

The roots of our faith are grounded in hearing the Word of God. For the first millennium of Christianity, the reciting of Holy Scripture was the primary method of conveying God's Word to the people. They would listen, then ponder what God was saying to them.

Reading the Word out loud continued in monasteries even after Scripture was copied onto pages and put into books. One monk saw a parallel between the rhythm of daily life and their spiritual exercises. In the same way the monks cultivated the land, they cultivated Scripture to bring forth fruit in their lives. Reading, meditation, prayer, and contemplation were the rungs of a ladder lifting them from earth to touch the secrets of heaven. This form of devotional reading became known as *Lectio Divina*, which is Latin for divine reading of Scripture.

Divine reading of Scripture simply means to read it in the context of personal prayer. We talk to God when we pray, but reading devotionally is our opportunity to listen to what he wants to say. God's Word is his love letter to us. It inspires, exhorts, and encourages us every time we interact with it. Praying Scripture out loud awakens our senses and readies us to respond.

David Benner, in his book *Opening to God*, calls Lectio Divina "…the prayer of listening, watching, waiting and seeking to discern the presence of the God who is not only always present but also always reaching out to us in love."

In order to listen to what God is saying, we must slow down. The four steps of Lectio Divina fall naturally into place with the Rosary, and the beads keep us grounded and focused throughout the practice.

The process begins by taking a small selection of Scripture and gently reciting it with an open awareness to the Holy Spirit. Then the Scripture is read again while pondering what we see, hear, or feel, and how it applies personally. Prayer is next as we respond to what's been brought to our attention, which then leads us to the final portion of Lectio Divina: contemplation and communion with God.

The intent of devotional reading is relationship. Moving through the pattern of the Rosary we wait upon the Lord to reveal himself by stirring our hearts, impressing our wills, and enlightening our minds. The movements of the Spirit can be subtle. The more we engage with the practice, the easier it will be to discern what God is saying to us. Ultimately, we trust God's grace is working in and through us regardless of the depth of our experience.

How to Pray this Rosary

First, choose a short portion of Scripture to meditate on. The Psalms are a good place to start because they naturally lend themselves to prayer and meditation. Encompassing the throes of human experience, the Psalms give voice to the deepest desires of our hearts. That said, all Scripture is worthy of our attention, and God speaks to us throughout the Bible. The idea here is to keep the reading somewhat short because you will be repeating it several times. You can read the New Testament or any of the books in the Old Testament this way as long as you break them into small portions.

Another option for finding a reading is to choose one of the Daily Scriptures from the Lectionary in this book. Or, you can use a devotional book and go deeper with the Scripture reference it provides. How you select a reading isn't important, as long as the portion is not too long for the time you have to spend with it.

The Anglican Rosary

Sit in a comfortable, quiet spot and place the chosen reading in your lap. Holding the cross on your Rosary, begin by placing yourself in God's presence. Because the concepts of Lectio Divina can be initially challenging, the instructions for each step of praying this way are included in the Rosary.

Lectio Divina Rosary

CROSS

Psalm 25:1, 2, 5

Take a moment to breathe deeply and slowly. Sit in silence and place your awareness on your heart, knowing that God is here with you. Pray the opening prayer.

> To you, O Lord, I lift up my soul.
>   O my God, in you I trust.
>   Let me not be put to shame;
>   Let not my enemies exult over me.
> Lead me in your truth and teach me,
>   For you are the God of my salvation.

INVITATORY

Psalm 95:1-2, 19

Recite Psalm 95 slowly and meaningfully, with the intention to listen and receive from God's Word.

> Oh come, let us sing to the Lord;
>   let us make a joyful noise to the rock of our salvation!
> Let us come into his presence with thanksgiving;
>   let us make a joyful noise to him with songs of praise!
> Open to me the gates of righteousness,
>   that I may enter through them
>   and give thanks to the Lord.

CRUCIFORM 1 — Reading

Read your selected Scripture out loud, paying close attention to each word and phrase. Listen for a word or portion that jumps out, or piques your curiosity. These slight promptings are the Holy Spirit's way of getting our attention.

WEEK

Take the word or phrase that you noticed from the reading and recite it on each of the seven beads as you open your heart to receive what God is trying to bring to your attention.

CRUCIFORM 2 — Meditation

Read the same Scripture again, savoring each word and phrase. Reflect on what God might be saying to you as you ponder how this applies to your life.

WEEK

Say the same word or phrase, or a different one if prompted, on the week beads, allowing the word to speak to you. Be aware of impressions that come in the form of memories, ideas, or concerns. You might see a picture in your mind, or, remember something that was said to you. What is the Holy Spirit bringing to your attention?

CRUCIFORM 3 — Prayer

Pray before you recite the Scripture for the third time. Ask for insight and understanding why this may be important to you today. Now read the Scripture again.

WEEK

Respond. The next seven beads offer time and space to respond to what you are experiencing through your interaction with this Scripture. There is no set formula. Pray from your heart. Are you confused? Tell God. Did something surface from your past? Give it to him. Did he give you insight? Thank him. Move through the beads intuitively taking as much time as you need. God loves and accepts you, talk to him about what you believe he is revealing to you through his Word.

CRUCIFORM 4 – Contemplation

Rest in God's embrace as you read the Scripture for the final time. Let the Word wash over you, releasing all unnecessary thought. Allow whatever experience you've had to come together not by your own effort, but through God's grace.

WEEK

Receive. These final week beads are a time of receiving and reflecting. What have you learned as a result of this time with God's Word? How will you act differently? Has your perception of yourself or who God is changed? What does this mean going forward? Trust that God is working in your life as you recite the following prayer from Psalm 85 on each bead.

Psalm 85:8

> I will listen to what the Lord God is saying, he speaks peace to those who are faithful.

CRUCIFORM 1

Psalm 19:14

> Let the words of my mouth and the meditation of my heart be acceptable in your sight, O Lord, my rock and my redeemer.

INVITATORY

Jude 24;25

> Now to him who is able to keep you from stumbling and to present you blameless before the presence of his glory with great joy, to the only God, our Savior, through Jesus Christ our Lord, be glory, majesty, dominion, and authority, before all time and now and forever. Amen.

CROSS

> Glory to the Father, and to the Son, and to the Holy Spirit: as it was in the beginning, is now, and will be forever. Amen.

~9~
Daily Scripture Readings

Thy word is a lamp unto my feet, and a light unto my path.
—*Psalm 119:105 (KJB)*

Reading the Bible is a vital part of our walk with God. We are encouraged to be in the Word on a daily basis. As we navigate the unpredictable waters of life, scripture anchors our soul in the heavenly realm where the grace of God resides. When we combine scriptural reading with the Rosary the Word of God takes root in our hearts, enabling the Holy Spirit to bear fruit in our lives.

The ACNA[7] Daily Office Lectionary is a collection of scripture readings appointed for each day of the year. The readings for Sunday services, Holy Days, and Morning and Evening prayer are found here. However, the Lectionary also provides the perfect guide for reading through the Bible in two years. The following pages offer a simple adaptation of the Lectionary for this purpose.

The Lectionary follows the days of the calendar year which makes it easy to drop in spontaneously or pick back up if you take a break. The two-year cycle begins in odd-numbered years (e.g., 2019) with the readings listed in Year One. Even-numbered years (e.g., 2020) readings are found in Year Two. In this way, we journey through the Word with other believers regardless of time and space.

Each day's readings include selections from the Old and New Testaments, and one or more Psalms. Readings may vary on Holy Days (Christmas, Easter, etc.), but in general, they move consecutively

---

[7] Anglican Church in North America

through each book. Following this guide for two years takes us through the entire New Testament twice (once each year) and the Old Testament once. Included in the readings are a few selections from the Apocrypha (writings not part of the standard Bible that are good examples of life and instruction of manners[8]). Some of the longer readings have shorter options which are listed with a cross (†) if time is an issue. Also, a few passages in the Old Testament have been left out for the sake of brevity.

How To Pray This Rosary

The Rosary is a template for moving through the readings in a meditative state. The scriptures for each day are divided between the four Cruciforms. The classic Jesus Prayer—*Lord Jesus Christ, Son of God, have mercy on me, a sinner*—is prayed on the seven Week beads while contemplating the scripture reading.

The Jesus Prayer has been used since the sixth century to bring Christians into a closer relationship with God. This short, impactful prayer evokes an attitude of humility, drawing us into God's presence as we contemplate his Word.

An alternative for the Week beads is to repeat a select portion of the scripture you just read.

Be mindful of promptings from the Holy Spirit as you spend time in the Word. One scripture might grab your attention and lead you to explore other portions of the Bible, or it might speak to your heart and you'll want to focus solely on that scripture instead of finishing the assigned readings. The key is to pay attention to what God is saying, or showing you, at that moment. God speaks through his Word into our lives encouraging, healing, and restoring us into right relationship with him so we might receive his abundant mercy and unconditional love.

---

8 Article VI of the Thirty-Nine Articles of Religion

Daily Scripture Rosary

CROSS
1 Peter 1:3

> Blessed be the God and Father of our Lord Jesus Christ! According to his great mercy, he has caused us to be born again to a living hope through the resurrection of Jesus Christ from the dead.

INVITATORY
Psalm 51:15, 10-12

> O Lord, open my lips,
>   and my mouth will declare your praise.
> Create in me a clean heart, O God,
>   and renew a right spirit within me.
> Cast me not away from your presence,
>   and take not your Holy Spirit from me.
> Restore to me the joy of your salvation,
>   and uphold me with a willing spirit.

CRUCIFORM 1
First Psalm listed for today.

WEEK
> Lord Jesus Christ, Son of God, have mercy on me a sinner.

CRUCIFORM 2
Old Testament reading for today.

WEEK
> Lord Jesus Christ, Son of God, have mercy on me a sinner.

CRUCIFORM 3
New Testament reading for today.
WEEK
> Lord Jesus Christ, Son of God, have mercy on me a sinner.

CRUCIFORM 4

Remaining Psalms for today, or re-read the first one.

WEEK

Lord Jesus Christ, Son of God, have mercy on me a sinner.

CRUCIFORM 1

The Lord's Prayer

Our Father, who art in heaven,
 hallowed be thy Name,
 thy kingdom come,
 thy will be done,
  on earth as it is in heaven.
Give us this day our daily bread.
And forgive us our trespasses,
 as we forgive those
  who trespass against us.
And lead us not into temptation,
 but deliver us from evil.
For thine is the kingdom,
 and the power, and the glory,
 for ever and ever. Amen.

INVITATORY

Lord God, almighty and everlasting Father, you have brought us in safety to this new day: Preserve us with your mighty power, that we may not fall into sin, nor be overcome by adversity; and in all we do, direct us to the fulfilling of your purpose; through Jesus Christ our Lord. Amen.

CROSS

Glory be to the Father, and to the Son, and to the Holy Spirit; as it was in the beginning, is now, and ever shall be, world without end. Amen.

Daily Office Lectionary Year One

Date	Old Testament	New Testament	Psalms
January 1	Gen 1	John 1:1-28	1, 2
January 2	Gen 2	John 1:29-end	5, 6
January 3	Gen 3	John 2	9
January 4	Gen 4	John 3:1-21	8, 11
January 5	Gen 5	John 3:22-end	12, 13, 14
January 6	Gen 6	Matt 2:1-12	96, 97
January 7	Gen 7	John 4:1-26	18:1-20v
January 8	Gen 8	John 4:27-end	19
January 9	Gen 9	John 5:1-24	22
January 10	Gen 10 † 1-9,15-22,30-32	John 5:25-end	25
January 11	Gen 11 † 1-9,27-32	John 6:1-21	26, 28
January 12	Gen 12	John 6:22-40	29, 30
January 13	Gen 13	John 6:41-end	34
January 14	Gen 14	John 7:1-24	32, 36
January 15	Gen 15	John 7:25-52	37:1-18v
January 16	Gen 16	John 7:53—8:30	40
January 17	Gen 17	John 8:31-end	42, 43
January 18	Gen 18	Matt 16:13-20	45
January 19	Gen 19 † 1-29	John 9	47, 48
January 20	Gen 20	John 10:1-21	50
January 21	Gen 21 † 1-21	John 10:22-end	52, 53, 54
January 22	Gen 22	John 11:1-44	56, 57
January 23	Gen 23	John 11:45-end	59
January 24	Gen 24 † 1-28,53-58	John 12:1-19	61, 62
January 25	Acts 9:1-22	John 12:20-end	68:1-18
January 26	Gen 25 † 7-11,19-34	John 13	69:1-18v
January 27	Gen 26 † 1-25	John 14:1-14	66
January 28	Gen 27 † 1-13,18-36,39-40	John 14:15-end	71

Date	Old Testament	New Testament	Psalms
January 29	Gen 28	John 15:1-17	74
January 30	Gen 29 † 1-28	John 15:18-end	75, 76
January 31	Gen 30 † 1-2,22-43	John 16:1-15	78:1-18v
February 1	Gen 31 † 1-3,17-45	John 16:16-end	78:41-73v
February 2	Gen 32 † 1-13,21-32	Luke 2:22-40	24, 81
February 3	Gen 33	John 17	83
February 4	Gen 34	John 18:1-27	86, 87
February 5	Gen 35	John 18:28-end	89:1-18v
February 6	Gen 36 † 1-8	John 19:1-37	90
February 7	Gen 37 † 3-8,12-36	John 19:38-end	92, 93
February 8	Gen 38 † 1-26	John 20	95, 96
February 9	Gen 39	John 21	99, 100, 101
February 10	Gen 40	Matt 1:1-17	103
February 11	Gen 41 † 1-15,25-40	Matt 1:18-end	105:1-22v
February 12	Gen 42 † 1-28	Matt 2	106:1-18v
February 13	Gen 43 † 1-10,15-34	Matt 3	107:1-22
February 14	Gen 44 † 1-20,30-34	Matt 4	108, 110
February 15	Gen 45	Matt 5:1-20	111, 112
February 16	Gen 46 † 1-7,28-34	Matt 5:21-48	115
February 17	Gen 47 † 1-15,23-31	Matt 6:1-18	119:1-24
February 18	Gen 48	Matt 6:19-end	119:49-72
February 19	Gen 49	Matt 7	119:89-104
February 20	Gen 50	Matt 8:1-17	119:129-152
February 21	Exod 1	Matt 8:18-end	118
February 22	Exod 2	Matt 9:1-17	122, 123
February 23	Exod 3	Matt 9:18-34	127, 128
February 24	Acts 1:15-26	Matt 9:35—10:23	132, 133
February 25	Exod 4	Matt 10:24-end	136
February 26	Exod 5	Matt 11	139
February 27	Exod 6 † 1-13	Matt 12:1-21	140
February 28	Exod 7	Matt 12:22-end	144

The Anglican Rosary

Date	Old Testament	New Testament	Psalms
February 29	2 Kings 2	Luke 24:44-53	90
March 1	Exod 8	Matt 13:1-23	146
March 2	Exod 9 † 1-29,33-34	Matt 13:24-43	148
March 3	Exod 10	Matt 13:44-end	1, 2
March 4	Exod 11	Matt 14	5, 6
March 5	Exod 12 † 1-20,28-36	Matt 15:1-28	9
March 6	Exod 13	Matt 15:29—16:12	8, 11
March 7	Exod 14 † 5-31	Matt 16:13-end	12, 13, 14
March 8	Exod 15	Matt 17:1-23	18:1-20v
March 9	Exod 16 † 1-7,11-33	Matt 17:24—18:14	19
March 10	Exod 17	Matt 18:15-end	22
March 11	Exod 18	Matt 19:1-15	25
March 12	Exod 19	Matt 19:16—20:16	26, 28
March 13	Exod 20	Matt 20:17-end	29, 30
March 14	Exod 21 † 1-19,22-29	Matt 21:1-22	34
March 15	Exod 22	Matt 21:23-end	32, 36
March 16	Exod 23 † 1-13,18-30	Matt 22:1-33	37:1-18v
March 17	Exod 24	Matt 22:34—23:12	40
March 18	Exod 25 † 1-23,31-40	Matt 23:13-end	42, 43
March 19	Exod 26 † 1-10,15-16,29-37	Matt 24:1-28	45
March 20	Exod 27	Matt 24:29-end	47, 48
March 21	Exod 28 † 1-6,15-21, 29-43	Matt 25:1-30	50
March 22	Exod 29 † 1-18,35-46	Matt 25:31-end	52, 53, 54
March 23	Exod 30 † 1-3,7-33	Matt 26:1-30	56, 57
March 24	Exod 31	Matt 26:31-56	59
March 25	Exod 32 † 1-29	Luke 1:26-38	113, 138
March 26	Exod 33	Matt 26:57-end	61, 62
March 27	Exod 34 † 1-17,27-35	Matt 27:1-26	68:1-18
March 28	Exod 35 † 1-10,20-35	Matt 27:27-56	69:1-18v
March 29	Exod 36 † 1-10,18-20, 31-38	Matt 27:57—28 end	66
March 30	Exod 37 † 1-11,16-29	Mark 1:1-13	71

Year One

Date	Old Testament	New Testament	Psalms
March 31	Exod 38 † 1-23	Mark 1:14-31	74
April 1	Exod 39 † 1-14,27-43	Mark 1:32-end	75, 76
April 2	Exod 40 † 1,16-38	Mark 2:1-22	78:1-18v
April 3	Lev 1	Mark 2:23—3:12	78:41-73v
April 4	Lev 8 † 1-24,30-36	Mark 3:13-end	81
April 5	Lev 10	Mark 4:1-34	84
April 6	Lev 16 † 1-22,29-34	Mark 4:35—5:20	86, 87
April 7	Lev 17	Mark 5:21-end	89:1-18v
April 8	Lev 18	Mark 6:1-29	90
April 9	Lev 19 † 1-2,9-37	Mark 6:30-end	92, 93
April 10	Lev 20	Mark 7:1-23	95, 96
April 11	Lev 23 † 9-32,39-43	Mark 7:24—8:10	99, 100, 101
April 12	Lev 26 † 3-20,38-46	Mark 8:11-end	103
April 13	Num 6	Mark 9:1-29	105:1-22v
April 14	Num 8 † 5-26	Mark 9:30-end	106:1-18v
April 15	Num 11 † 4-6,10-33	Mark 10:1-31	107:1-22
April 16	Num 12	Mark 10:32-end	108, 110
April 17	Num 13 † 1-3,17-33	Mark 11:1-26	111, 112
April 18	Num 14 † 1-31	Mark 11:27—12:12	115
April 19	Num 15 † 22-41	Mark 12:13-34	119:1-24
April 20	Num 16 † 1-11,20-38	Mark 12:35—13:13	119:49-72
April 21	Num 17	Mark 13:14-end	119:89-104
April 22	Num 18 † 1-24	Mark 14:1-25	119:129-152
April 23	Num 20	Mark 14:26-52	118
April 24	Num 21 † 4-9,21-35	Mark 14:53-end	122, 123
April 25	Acts 12:11-25	Mark 15	127, 128
April 26	Num 22 † 1-35	Mark 16	132, 133
April 27	Num 23 † 1-26	Luke 1:1-23	136
April 28	Num 24	Luke 1:24-56	139
April 29	Num 25	Luke 1:57-end	140
April 30	Deut 1 † 1-21,26-33	Luke 2:1-21	144

The Anglican Rosary

Date	Old Testament	New Testament	Psalms
May 1	Deut 2 † 1-9,14-19,24-37	Luke 2:22-end	146
May 2	Deut 3	Luke 3:1-22	148
May 3	Deut 4 † 1-18,24-40	Luke 3:23-end	1, 2
May 4	Deut 5	Luke 4:1-30	5, 6
May 5	Deut 6	Luke 4:31-end	9
May 6	Deut 7	Luke 5:1-16	8, 11
May 7	Deut 8	Luke 5:17-end	12, 13, 14
May 8	Deut 9	Luke 6:1-19	18:1-20v
May 9	Deut 10	Luke 6:20-38	19
May 10	Deut 11	Luke 6:39—7:10	22
May 11	Deut 12	Luke 7:11-35	25
May 12	Deut 13	Luke 7:36-end	26, 28
May 13	Deut 14	Luke 8:1-21	29, 30
May 14	Deut 15	Luke 8:22-end	34
May 15	Deut 16	Luke 9:1-17	32, 36
May 16	Deut 17	Luke 9:18-50	37:1-18v
May 17	Deut 18	Luke 9:51-end	40
May 18	Deut 19	Luke 10:1-24	42, 43
May 19	Deut 20	Luke 10:25-end	45
May 20	Deut 21	Luke 11:1-28	47, 48
May 21	Deut 22	Luke 11:29-end	50
May 22	Deut 23	Luke 12:1-34	52, 53, 54
May 23	Deut 24	Luke 12:35-53	56, 57
May 24	Deut 25	Luke 12:54—13:9	59
May 25	Deut 26	Luke 13:10-end	61, 62
May 26	Deut 27	Luke 14:1-24	68:1-18
May 27	Deut 28 † 1-25,64-68	Luke 14:25—15:10	69:1-18v
May 28	Deut 29	Luke 15:11-end	66
May 29	Deut 30	Luke 16	71
May 30	Deut 31	Luke 17:1-19	74
May 31	Deut 32 † 1-10,15-22,39-52	Luke 1:39-56	75, 76
June 1	Deut 33	Luke 17:20-end	78:1-18v
June 2	Deut 34	Luke 18:1-30	78:41-73v

Year One

Date	Old Testament	New Testament	Psalms
June 3	Josh 1	Luke 18:31—19:10	81
June 4	Josh 2	Luke 19:11-28	84
June 5	Josh 3	Luke 19:29-end	86, 87
June 6	Josh 4	Luke 20:1-26	89:1-18v
June 7	Josh 5	Luke 20:27—21:4	90
June 8	Josh 6	Luke 21:5-end	92, 93
June 9	Josh 7	Luke 22:1-38	95, 96
June 10	Josh 8 † 1-22,30-35	Luke 22:39-53	99, 100, 101
June 11	Acts 4:32-37	Luke 22:54-end	103
June 12	Josh 9	Luke 23:1-25	105:1-22v
June 13	Josh 10 † 1-27,40-43	Luke:23:26-49	106:1-18v
June 14	Josh 14 † 5-15	Luke 23:50—24:12	107:1-22
June 15	Josh 22 † 7-31	Luke 24:13-end	108, 110
June 16	Josh 23	Gal 1	111, 112
June 17	Josh 24 † 1-31	Gal 2	115
June 18	Judg 1 † 1-21	Gal 3	119:1-24
June 19	Judg 2 † 6-23	Gal 4	119:49-72
June 20	Judg 3 † 7-30	Gal 5	119:89-104
June 21	Judg 4	Gal 6	119:129-152
June 22	Judg 5 † 1-5,19-31	1 Thess 1	118
June 23	Judg 6 † 1,6,11-24,33-40	1 Thess 2:1-16	122, 123
June 24	1 Thess 2:17—3 end	Matt 14:1-13	127, 128
June 25	Judg 7 † 1-8,16-25	1 Thess 4:1-12	132, 133
June 26	Judg 8 † 4-23,28	1 Thess 4:13—5:11	136
June 27	Judg 9 † 1-6,22-25,43-56	1 Thess 5:12-end	139
June 28	Judg 10 † 6-18	2 Thess 1	140
June 29	2 Thess 2	2 Pet 3:14-end	144
June 30	Judg 11 † 1-11,29-40	2 Thess 3	146
July 1	Judg 12	1 Cor 1:1-25	148
July 2	Judg 13	1 Cor 1:26—2 end	1, 2
July 3	Judg 14	1 Cor 3	5, 6

The Anglican Rosary

Date	Old Testament	New Testament	Psalms
July 4	Judg 15	1 Cor 4:1-17	9
July 5	Judg 16	1 Cor 4:18—5 end	8, 11
July 6	Ruth 1	1 Cor 6	12, 13, 14
July 7	Ruth 2	1 Cor 7	18:1-20v
July 8	Ruth 3	1 Cor 8	19
July 9	Ruth 4	1 Cor 9	22
July 10	1 Sam 1 † 1-20	1 Cor 10	25
July 11	1 Sam 2 † 1-21	1 Cor 11	26, 28
July 12	1 Sam 3	1 Cor 12	29, 30
July 13	1 Sam 4	1 Cor 13	34
July 14	1 Sam 5	1 Cor 14:1-19	32, 36
July 15	1 Sam 6 † 1-15	1 Cor 14:20-end	37:1-18v
July 16	1 Sam 7	1 Cor 15:1-34	40
July 17	1 Sam 8	1 Cor 15:35-end	42, 43
July 18	1 Sam 9	1 Cor 16	45
July 19	1 Sam 10	2 Cor 1:1—2:11	47, 48
July 20	1 Sam 11	2 Cor 2:12—3 end	50
July 21	1 Sam 12	2 Cor 4	52, 53, 54
July 22	2 Cor 5	Luke 7:36—8:3	56, 57
July 23	1 Sam 13	2 Cor 6	59
July 24	1 Sam 14 † 1-15,20,24-30	2 Cor 7	61, 62
July 25	2 Cor 8	Mark 1:14-20	68:1-18
July 26	1 Sam 15	2 Cor 9	69:1-18v
July 27	1 Sam 16	2 Cor 10	66
July 28	1 Sam 17 † 1-11,26-27,31-51	2 Cor 11	71
July 29	1 Sam 18	2 Cor 12:1-13	74
July 30	1 Sam 19	2 Cor 12:14—13 end	75, 76
July 31	1 Sam 20 † 1-7,24-42	Rom 1	78:1-18v
August 1	1 Sam 21	Rom 2	78:41-73v
August 2	1 Sam 22	Rom 3	81
August 3	1 Sam 23	Rom 4	84

Year One

Date	Old Testament	New Testament	Psalms
August 4	1 Sam 24	Rom 5	86, 87
August 5	1 Sam 25 † 1-19,23-25,32-42	Rom 6	89:1-18v
August 6	Rom 7	Mark 9:2-10	27
August 7	1 Sam 26	Rom 8:1-17	90
August 8	1 Sam 27	Rom 8:18-end	92, 93
August 9	1 Sam 28	Rom 9	95, 96
August 10	1 Sam 29	Rom 10	99, 100, 101
August 11	1 Sam 30 † 1-25	Rom 11	103
August 12	1 Sam 31	Rom 12	105:1-22v
August 13	2 Sam 1	Rom 13	106:1-18v
August 14	2 Sam 2 † 1-17,26-31	Rom 14	107:1-22
August 15	2 Sam 3 † 6-11,17-39	Luke 1:26-38	108, 110
August 16	2 Sam 4	Rom 15	111, 112
August 17	2 Sam 5	Rom 16	115
August 18	2 Sam 6	Phil 1:1-11	119:1-24
August 19	2 Sam 7	Phil 1:12-end	119:49-72
August 20	2 Sam 8	Phil 2:1-11	119:89-104
August 21	2 Sam 9	Phil 2:12-end	119:129-152
August 22	2 Sam 10	Phil 3	118
August 23	2 Sam 11	Phil 4	122, 123
August 24	Col 1:1-20	Luke 6:12-16	127, 128
August 25	2 Sam 12 † 1-25	Col 1:21—2:7	132, 133
August 26	2 Sam 13 † 1-29,38-39	Col 2:8-19	136
August 27	2 Sam 14 † 1-21,28	Col 2:20—3:11	139
August 28	2 Sam 15 † 1-18,23-25,32-34	Col 3:12-end	140
August 29	2 Sam 16	Col 4	144
August 30	2 Sam 17 † 1-23	Philemon	146
August 31	2 Sam 18 † 1-15,19-33	Eph 1:1-14	148
Sept. 1	2 Sam 19 † 1-30	Eph 1:15-end	1, 2

The Anglican Rosary

Date	Old Testament	New Testament	Psalms
Sept. 2	2 Sam 20	Eph 2:1-10	5, 6
Sept. 3	2 Sam 21	Eph 2:11-end	9
Sept. 4	2 Sam 22 † 1-7,14-20,32-51	Eph 3	8, 11
Sept. 5	2 Sam 23 † 1-23	Eph 4:1-16	12, 13, 14
Sept. 6	2 Sam 24	Eph 4:17-end	18:1-20v
Sept. 7	1 Chron 22	Eph 5:1-17	19
Sept. 8	1 Kings 1 † 1-18,29-40	Eph 5:18-end	22
Sept. 9	1 Chron 28	Eph 6	25
Sept. 10	1 Kings 2 † 1-25	Heb 1	26, 28
Sept. 11	1 Kings 3	Heb 2	29, 30
Sept. 12	1 Kings 4 † 1-6,20-34	Heb 3	34
Sept. 13	1 Kings 5	Heb 4:1-13	32, 36
Sept. 14	Heb 4:14—5:10	John 12:23-33	37:1-18v
Sept. 15	1 Kings 6 † 1-7,11-30,37-38	Heb 5:11—6 end	40
Sept. 16	1 Kings 7 † 1-14,40-44,47-51	Heb 7	42, 43
Sept. 17	1 Kings 8 † 1-11,22-30,54-63	Heb 8	45
Sept. 18	1 Kings 9 † 1-9,15-28	Heb 9:1-14	47, 48
Sept. 19	1 Kings 10 †1-13,23-29	Heb 9:15-end	50
Sept. 20	1 Kings 11 † 1-14,23-33,41-43	Heb 10:1-18	52, 53, 54
Sept. 21	Heb 10:19-end	Matt 9:9-13	56, 57
Sept. 22	1 Kings 12 † 1-20,25-30	Heb 11	59
Sept. 23	1 Kings 13 † 1-25,33-34	Heb 12:1-17	61, 62
Sept. 24	1 Kings 14	Heb 12:18-end	68:1-18
Sept. 25	2 Chron 12	Heb 13	69:1-18v
Sept. 26	2 Chron 13	Jas 1	66
Sept. 27	2 Chron 14	Jas 2:1-13	71
Sept. 28	2 Chron 15	Jas 2:14-end	74
Sept. 29	Rev 12:7-12	Jas 3	75, 76
Sept. 30	2 Chron 16	Jas 4	78:1-18v

Year One

Date	Old Testament	New Testament	Psalms
October 1	1 Kings 15 † 1-30	Jas 5	78:41-73v
October 2	1 Kings 16 † 1-4,8-19,23-34	1 Pet 1:1-21	81
October 3	1 Kings 17	1 Pet 1:22—2:10	84
October 4	1 Kings 18 † 1-8,17-46	1 Pet 2:11—3:7	86, 87
October 5	1 Kings 19	1 Pet 3:8—4:6	89:1-18v
October 6	1 Kings 20 † 1,13,21-43	1 Pet 4:7-end	90
October 7	1 Kings 21	1 Pet 5	92, 93
October 8	1 Kings 22 † 1-23,29-38	2 Pet 1	95, 96
October 9	2 Chron 20	2 Pet 2	99, 100, 101
October 10	2 Kings 1	2 Pet 3	103
October 11	2 Kings 2	Jude	105:1-22v
October 12	2 Kings 3	1 John 1:1—2:6	106:1-18v
October 13	2 Kings 4 † 8-37	1 John 2:7-end	107:1-22
October 14	2 Kings 5	1 John 3:1-10	108, 110
October 15	2 Kings 6 † 1-24	1 John 3:11—4:6	111, 112
October 16	2 Kings 7	1 John 4:7-end	115
October 17	2 Kings 8 † 1-19,25-27	1 John 5	119:1-24
October 18	2 John	Luke 1:1-4	119:49-72
October 19	2 Kings 9 † 1-26,30-37	3 John	119:89-104
October 20	2 Kings 10 † 1-11,18-31	Acts 1:1-14	119:129-152
October 21	2 Kings 11 † 1-16,23-27	Acts 1:15-end	118
October 22	2 Kings 12	Acts 2:1-21	122, 123
October 23	Acts 2:22-end	James 1	127, 128
October 24	2 Kings 13	Acts 3:1—4:4	132, 133
October 25	2 Kings 14	Acts 4:5-31	136
October 26	2 Chron 26	Acts 4:32—5:11	139
October 27	2 Kings 15 † 1-29	Acts 5:12-end	140
October 28	Acts 6:1—7:16	John 14:15-31	144
October 29	2 Kings 16	Acts 7:17-34	146
October 30	2 Kings 17 † 1-28,41	Acts 7:35—8:3	148

The Anglican Rosary

Date	Old Testament	New Testament	Psalms
October 31	2 Chron 28	Acts 8:4-25	2
Nov. 1	Heb 11:32—12:2	Acts 8:26-end	1, 15
Nov. 2	2 Chron 29 † 1-11,20-30,35-36	Acts 9:1-31	5, 6
Nov. 3	2 Chron 30 † 1-22,26-27	Acts 9:32-end	9
Nov. 4	2 Kings 18 † 1-13,17-30,35-37	Acts 10:1-23	8, 11
Nov. 5	2 Kings 19 † 1-20,29-31,35-37	Acts 10:24-end	12, 13, 14
Nov. 6	2 Kings 20	Acts 11:1-18	18:1-20v
Nov. 7	2 Chron 33	Acts 11:19-end	19
Nov. 8	2 Kings 21	Acts 12:1-24	22
Nov. 9	2 Kings 22	Acts 12:25—13:12	25
Nov. 10	2 Kings 23 † 1-20,26-30	Acts 13:13-43	26, 28
Nov. 11	2 Kings 24	Acts 13:44—14:7	29, 30
Nov. 12	2 Kings 25 † 1-22,25-30	Acts 14:8-end	34
Nov. 13	Judith 4	Acts 15:1-21	32, 36
Nov. 14	Judith 8	Acts 15:22-35	37:1-18v
Nov. 15	Judith 9	Acts 15:36—16:5	40
Nov. 16	Judith 10	Acts 16:6-end	42, 43
Nov. 17	Judith 11	Acts 17:1-15	45
Nov. 18	Judith 12	Acts 17:16-end	47, 48
Nov. 19	Judith 13	Acts 18:1-23	50
Nov. 20	Judith 14	Acts 18:24—19:7	52, 53, 54
Nov. 21	Judith 15	Acts 19:8-20	56, 57
Nov. 22	Judith 16	Acts 19:21-end	59
Nov. 23	Ecclesiasticus 1	Acts 20:1-16	61, 62
Nov. 24	Ecclesiasticus 2	Acts 20:17-end	68:1-18
Nov. 25	Ecclesiasticus 4 † 1-19	Acts 21:1-16	69:1-18v
Nov. 26	Ecclesiasticus 6 † 5-31	Acts 21:17-36	66
Nov. 27	Ecclesiasticus 7 † 1-21,27-36	Acts 21:37—22:22	71
Nov. 28	Ecclesiasticus 9	Acts 22:23—23:11	74
Nov. 29	Ecclesiasticus 10 † 1-24	Acts 23:12-end	75, 76

Year One

Date	Old Testament	New Testament	Psalms
Nov. 30	Ecclesiasticus 11 † 1-9,18-28	John 1:35-42	78:1-18v
Dec. 1	Ecclesiasticus 14	Acts 24:1-23	78:41-73v
Dec. 2	Ecclesiasticus 17	Acts 24:24—25:12	81
Dec. 3	Ecclesiasticus 18 † 1-26,30-33	Acts 25:13-end	84
Dec. 4	Ecclesiasticus 21	Acts 26	86, 87
Dec. 5	Ecclesiasticus 34	Acts 27	89:1-18v
Dec. 6	Ecclesiasticus 38 † 1-15,24-34	Acts 28:1-15	90
Dec. 7	Ecclesiasticus 39 † 1-11,16-35	Acts 28:16-end	92, 93
Dec. 8	Ecclesiasticus 44	Rev 1	95, 96
Dec. 9	Ecclesiasticus 45	Rev 2:1-17	99, 100, 101
Dec. 10	Ecclesiasticus 46	Rev 2:18—3:6	103
Dec. 11	Ecclesiasticus 47	Rev 3:7-end	105:1-22v
Dec. 12	Ecclesiasticus 48	Rev 4	106:1-18v
Dec. 13	Ecclesiasticus 49	Rev 5	107:1-22
Dec. 14	Ecclesiasticus 50	Rev 6	108, 110
Dec. 15	Ecclesiasticus 51	Rev 7	111, 112
Dec. 16	Wisdom 1	Rev 8	115
Dec. 17	Wisdom 2	Rev 9	119:1-24
Dec. 18	Wisdom 3	Rev 10	119:49-72
Dec. 19	Wisdom 4	Rev 11	119:89-104
Dec. 20	Wisdom 5	Rev 12	119:129-152
Dec. 21	Rev 13	John 14:1-7	118
Dec. 22	Wisdom 6	Rev 14	122, 123
Dec. 23	Wisdom 7	Rev 15	127, 128
Dec. 24	Wisdom 8	Rev 16	132, 133
Dec. 25	Isa 9:1-8	Rev 17	19 or 45
Dec. 26	Acts 6:8—7:6, 7:44-60	Rev 18	136

The Anglican Rosary

Date	Old Testament	New Testament	Psalms
Dec. 27	Rev 19	John 21:9-25	139
Dec. 28	Jer 31:1-17	Rev 20	140
Dec. 29	Wisdom 9	Rev 21:1-14	144
Dec. 30	Wisdom 10	Rev 21:15—22:5	146
Dec. 31	Wisdom 11	Rev 22:6-end	148

Daily Office Lectionary Year Two

Psalm	Date	Old Testament	New Testament
3, 4	January 1	Gal 1	Luke 2:8-21
7	January 2	Jer 1	Gal 2
10	January 3	Jer 2 † 1-22	Gal 3
15, 16	January 4	Jer 3	Gal 4
17	January 5	Jer 4	Gal 5
67, 72	January 6	Jer 5	John 2:1-12
18:21-50v	January 7	Jer 6	Gal 6
20, 21	January 8	Jer 7 † 1-28,34	1 Thess 1
23, 24	January 9	Jer 8	1 Thess 2:1-16
27	January 10	Jer 9	1 Thess 2:17—3 end
31	January 11	Jer 10	1 Thess 4:1-12
33	January 12	Jer 11	1 Thess 4:13—5:11
35	January 13	Jer 12	1 Thess 5:12-end
38	January 14	Jer 13	2 Thess 1
37:19-42v	January 15	Jer 14	2 Thess 2
39, 41	January 16	Jer 15	2 Thess 3
44	January 17	Jer 16	1 Cor 1:1-25
46	January 18r	Jer 17	1 Cor 1:26—2 end
49	January 19	Jer 18	1 Cor 3
51	January 20	Jer 19	1 Cor 4:1-17
55	January 21	Jer 20	1 Cor 4:18—5 end
58, 60	January 22	Jer 21	1 Cor 6
63, 64	January 23	Jer 22	1 Cor 7
65, 67	January 24	Jer 23 †1-9,16-18,21-40	1 Cor 8
68:19-36	January 25	Jer 24	1 Cor 9
69:19-38v	January 26	Jer 25 † 1-19,26-31	1 Cor 10
70, 72	January 27	Jer 26	1 Cor 11
73	January 28	Jer 27	1 Cor 12
77	January 29	Jer 28	1 Cor 13

The Anglican Rosary

Psalm	Date	Old Testament	New Testament
79, 82	January 30	Jer 29 † 1-14,24-32	1 Cor 14:1-19
78:19-40v	January 31	Jer 30	1 Cor 14:20-end
80	February 1	Jer 31 † 1-17,27-37	1 Cor 15:1-34
84	February 2	Jer 32 † 1-15,36-44	1 Cor 15:35-end
85	February 3	Jer 33	1 Cor 16
88	February 4	Jer 34	2 Cor 1:1—2:11
89:19-52v	February 5	Jer 35	2 Cor 2:12—3 end
91	February 6	Jer 36 † 1-10,19-32	2 Cor 4
94	February 7	Jer 37	2 Cor 5
97, 98	February 8	Jer 38	2 Cor 6
102	February 9	Jer 39	2 Cor 7
104	February 10	Jer 40	2 Cor 8
105:23-45v	February 11	Jer 41	2 Cor 9
106:19-48v	February 12	Jer 42	2 Cor 10
107:23-43	February 13	Jer 43	2 Cor 11
109	February 14	Jer 44 † 1-19,24-30	2 Cor 12:1-13
113, 114	February 15	Jer 45	2 Cor 12:14—13 end
116, 117	February 16	Jer 46	Rom 1
119:25-48	February 17	Jer 47	Rom 2
119:73-88	February 18	Jer 48 † 1-20,40-47	Rom 3
119:105-128	February 19	Jer 49 † 1-13,23-39	Rom 4
119:153-176	February 20	Jer 50 † 1-20,33-40	Rom 5
120, 121	February 21	Jer 51 † 6-10,45-64	Rom 6
124, 125, 126	February 22	Jer 52 † 1-27,31-34	Rom 7
129, 130, 131	February 23	Baruch 4 † 5-13,21-37	Rom 8:1-17
134, 135	February 24	Baruch 5	Rom 8:18-end
137, 138	February 25	Lam 1 † 1-12,17-22	Rom 9
141, 142	February 26	Lam 2 † 1-18	Rom 10
143	February 27	Lam 3 † 1-9,19-33,52-66	Rom 11
145	February 28	Lam 4	Rom 12

Year Two

Psalm	Date	Old Testament	New Testament
104	February 29	Joel 2 † 1-2,12-32	2 Pet 3
147	March 1	Lam 5	Rom 13
149, 150	March 2	Prov 1	Rom 14
3, 4	March 3	Prov 2	Rom 15
7	March 4	Prov 3 † 1-27	Rom 16
10	March 5	Prov 4	Phil 1:1-11
15, 16	March 6	Prov 5	Phil 1:12-end
17	March 7	Prov 6 † 1-11,20-35	Phil 2:1-11
18:21-50v	March 8	Prov 7	Phil 2:12-end
20, 21	March 9	Prov 8	Phil 3
23, 24	March 10	Prov 9	Phil 4
27	March 11	Prov 10	Col 1:1-20
31	March 12	Prov 11	Col 1:21—2:7
33	March 13	Prov 12	Col 2:8-19
35	March 14	Prov 13	Col 2:20—3:11
38	March 15	Prov 14	Col 3:12-end
37:19-42v	March 16	Prov 15	Col 4
39, 41	March 17	Prov 16	Philemon
44	March 18	Prov 17	Eph 1:1-14
46	March 19	Eph 1:15-end	Matt 1:18-26
49	March 20	Prov 18	Eph 2:1-10
51	March 21	Prov 19	Eph 2:11-end
55	March 22	Prov 20	Eph 3
58, 60	March 23	Prov 21	Eph 4:1-16
63, 64	March 24	Prov 22	Eph 4:17-end
131, 132	March 25	Prov 23	Eph 5:1-17
65, 67	March 26	Prov 24 † 1-14, 23-34	Eph 5:18-end
68:19-36	March 27	Prov 25	Eph 6:1-9
69:19-37	March 28	Prov 26	Eph 6:10-end
70, 72	March 29	Prov 27	1 Tim 1:1-17
73	March 30	Prov 28	1 Tim 1:18—2 end
77	March 31	Prov 29	1 Tim 3
79, 82	April 1	Prov 30 † 1-9,15-33	1 Tim 4

The Anglican Rosary

Psalm	Date	Old Testament	New Testament
78:19-40v	April 2	Prov 31	1 Tim 5
80	April 3	Job 1	1 Tim 6
83	April 4	Job 2	Titus 1
85	April 5	Job 3	Titus 2
88	April 6	Job 4	Titus 3
89:19-52v	April 7	Job 5	2 Tim 1
91	April 8	Job 6	2 Tim 2
94	April 9	Job 7	2 Tim 3
97, 98	April 10	Job 8	2 Tim 4
102	April 11	Job 9	Heb 1
104	April 12	Job 10	Heb 2
105:23-45v	April 13	Job 11	Heb 3
106:19-48v	April 14	Job 12	Heb 4:1-13
107:23-43	April 15	Job 13	Heb 4:14—5:10
109	April 16	Job 14	Heb 5:11—6 end
113, 114	April 17	Job 15	Heb 7
116, 117	April 18	Job 16	Heb 8
119:25-48	April 19	Job 17	Heb 9:1-14
119:73-88	April 20	Job 18	Heb 9:15-end
119:105-128	April 21	Job 19	Heb 10:1-18
119:153-176	April 22	Job 20	Heb 10:19-end
120, 121	April 23	Job 21	Heb 11
124, 125, 126	April 24	Job 22	Heb 12:1-17
129, 130, 131	April 25	Job 23	Heb 12:18-end
134, 135	April 26	Job 24	Heb 13
137, 138	April 27	Job 25 & 26	Jas 1
141, 142	April 28	Job 27	Jas 2:1-13
143	April 29	Job 28	Jas 2:14-end
145	April 30	Job 29	Jas 3
147	May 1.	Jas 4	John 1:43-end
149, 150	May 2	Job 30	Jas 5

Psalm	Date	Old Testament	New Testament
3, 4	May 3	Job 31 † 1-23,35-40	1 Pet 1:1-21
7	May 4	Job 32	1 Pet 1:22—2:10
10	May 5	Job 33	1 Pet 2:11—3:7
15, 16	May 6	Job 34 † 1-15,21-28,31-37	1 Pet 3:8—4:6
17	May 7	Job 35	1 Pet 4:7-end
18:21-50v	May 8	Job 36	1 Pet 5
20, 21	May 9	Job 37	2 Pet 1
23, 24	May 10	Job 38 † 1-27,31-33	2 Pet 2
27	May 11	Job 39	2 Pet 3
31	May 12	Job 40	Jude
33	May 13	Job 41	1 John 1:1—2:6
35	May 14	Job 42	1 John 2:7-end
38	May 15	Eccl 1	1 John 3:1-10
37:19-42v	May 16	Eccl 2	1 John 3:11—4:6
39, 41	May 17	Eccl 3	1 John 4:7-end
44	May 18	Eccl 4	1 John 5
46	May 19	Eccl 5	2 John
49	May 20	Eccl 6	3 John
51	May 21	Eccl 7	Acts 1:1-14
55	May 22	Eccl 8	Acts 1:15-end
58, 60	May 23	Eccl 9	Acts 2:1-21
63, 64	May 24	Eccl 10	Acts 2:22-end
65, 67	May 25	Eccl 11	Acts 3:1—4:4
68:19-36	May 26	Eccl 12	Acts 4:5-31
69:19-38v	May 27	Ezek 1	Acts 4:32—5:11
70, 72	May 28	Ezek 2	Acts 5:12-end
73	May 29	Ezek 3	Acts 6:1—7:16
77	May 30	Ezek 4	Acts 7:17-34
79, 82	May 31	Ezek 5	Acts 7:35—8:3
78:19-40v	June 1	Ezek 6	Acts 8:4-25
80	June 2	Ezek 7	Acts 8:26-end
83	June 3	Ezek 8	Acts 9:1-31

The Anglican Rosary

Psalm	Date	Old Testament	New Testament
85	June 4	Ezek 9	Acts 9:32-end
88	June 5	Ezek 10	Acts 10:1-23
89:19-52v	June 6	Ezek 11	Acts 10:24-end
91	June 7	Ezek 12	Acts 11:1-18
94	June 8	Ezek 13	Acts 11:19-end
97, 98	June 9	Ezek 14	Acts 12:1-24
102	June 10	Ezek 15	Acts 12:25—13:12
104	June 11	Ezek 16 † 1-15,33-47, 59-63	Acts 13:13-43
105:23-45v	June 12	Ezek 17	Acts 13:44—14:7
106:19-48v	June 13	Ezek 18	Acts 14:8-end
107:23-43	June 14	Ezek 33† 1-23,30-33	Acts 15:1-21
109	June 15	Ezek 34	Acts 15:22-35
113, 114	June 16	Ezek 35	Acts 15:36—16:5
116, 117	June 17	Ezek 36 † 16-37	Acts 16:6-end
119:25-48	June 18	Ezek 37	Acts 17:1-15
119:73-88	June 19	Ezek 40 † 1-5,17-19,35-49	Acts 17:16-end
119:105-128	June 20	Ezek 43	Acts 18:1-23
119:153-176	June 21	Ezek 47	Acts 18:24—19:7
120, 121	June 22	Dan 1	Acts 19:8-20
124, 125, 126	June 23	Dan 2 † 1-14,25-28,31-45	Acts 19:21-end
129, 130, 131	June 24	Dan 3	Acts 20:1-16
134, 135	June 25	Dan 4 † 1-9,19-35	Acts 20:17-end
137, 138	June 26	Dan 5	Acts 21:1-16
141, 142	June 27	Dan 6	Acts 21:17-36
143	June 28	Dan 7	Acts 21:37—22:22
145	June 29	Dan 8	Acts 22:23—23:11
147	June 30	Dan 9	Acts 23:12-end
149, 150	July 1	Dan 10	Acts 24:1-23
3, 4	July 2	Dan 11 † 1-19	Acts 24:24—25:12
7	July 3	Dan 12	Acts 25:13-end

Psalm	Date	Old Testament	New Testament
10	July 4	Susanna	Acts 26
15, 16	July 5	Esth 1	Acts 27
17	July 6	Esth 2	Acts 28:1-15
18:21-50v	July 7	Esth 3	Acts 28:16-end
20, 21	July 8	Esth 4	Philemon
23, 24	July 9	Esth 5	1 Tim 1:1-17
27	July 10	Esth 6	1 Tim 1:18—2 end
31	July 11	Esth 7	1 Tim 3
33	July 12	Esth 8	1 Tim 4
35	July 13	Esth 9 & 10	1 Tim 5
38	July 14	Ezra 1	1 Tim 6
37:19-42v	July 15	Ezra 3	Titus 1
39, 41	July 16	Ezra 4	Titus 2
44	July 17	Ezra 5	Titus 3
46	July 18	Ezra 6	2 Tim 1
49	July 19	Ezra 7	2 Tim 2
51	July 20	Ezra 8 † 21-36	2 Tim 3
55	July 21	Ezra 9	2 Tim 4
58, 60	July 22	Ezra 10 † 1-16	John 1:1-28
63, 64	July 23	Neh 1	John 1:29-end
65, 67	July 24	Neh 2	John 2
68:19-36	July 25	Neh 3 † 1-15	John 3:1-21
69:19-38v	July 26	Neh 4	John 3:22-end
70, 72	July 27	Neh 5	John 4:1-26
73	July 28	Neh 6	John 4:27-end
77	July 29	Neh 8	John 5:1-24
79, 82	July 30	Neh 9 † 1-15,26-38	John 5:25-end
78:19-40v	July 31	Neh 10 † 28-39	John 6:1-21
80	August 1	Neh 12 † 27-47	John 6:22-40
83	August 2	Neh 13 † 1-22,30-31	John 6:41-end
85	August 3	Hos 1	John 7:1-24
88	August 4	Hos 2	John 7:25-52
89:19-52v	August 5	Hos 3	John 7:53—8:30

The Anglican Rosary

Psalm	Date	Old Testament	New Testament
80	August 6	Hos 4	John 8:31-end
91	August 7	Hos 5	John 9
94	August 8	Hos 6	John 10:1-21
97, 98	August 9	Hos 7	John 10:22-end
102	August 10	Hos 8	John 11:1-44
104	August 11	Hos 9	John 11:45-end
105:23-45v	August 12	Hos 10	John 12:1-19
106:19-48v	August 13	Hos 11	John 12:20-end
107:23-43	August 14	Hos 12	John 13
109	August 15	Hos 13	John 14:1-14
113, 114	August 16	Hos 14	John 14:15-end
116, 117	August 17	Joel 1	John 15:1-17
119:25-48	August 18	Joel 2 † 1-17,28-32	John 15:18-end
119:73-88	August 19	Joel 3	John 16:1-15
119:105-128	August 20	Amos 1	John 16:16-end
119:153-176	August 21	Amos 2	John 17
120, 121	August 22	Amos 3	John 18:1-27
124, 125, 126	August 23	Amos 4	John 18:28-end
129, 130, 131	August 24	Amos 5	John 19:1-37
134, 135	August 25	Amos 6	John 19:38-end
137, 138	August 26	Amos 7	John 20
141, 142	August 27	Amos 8	John 21
143	August 28	Amos 9	Matt 1:1-17
145	August 29	Obadiah	Matt 1:18-end
147	August 30	Jonah 1	Matt 2
149, 150	August 31	Jonah 2	Matt 3
3, 4	Sept. 1	Jonah 3	Matt 4
7	Sept. 2	Jonah 4	Matt 5:1-20
10	Sept. 3	Mic 1	Matt 5:21-48
15, 16	Sept. 4	Mic 2	Matt 6:1-18
17	Sept. 5	Mic 3	Matt 6:19-end

Year Two

Psalm	Date	Old Testament	New Testament
18:21-50v	Sept. 6	Mic 4	Matt 7
20, 21	Sept. 7	Mic 5	Matt 8:1-17
23, 24	Sept. 8	Mic 6	Matt 8:18-end
27	Sept. 9	Mic 7	Matt 9:1-17
31	Sept. 10	Nahum 1	Matt 9:18-34
33	Sept. 11	Nahum 2	Matt 9:35—10:23
35	Sept. 12	Nahum 3	Matt 10:24-end
38	Sept. 13	Hab 1	Matt 11
37:19-42v	Sept. 14	Hab 2	Matt 12:1-21
39, 41	Sept. 15	Hab 3	Matt 12:22-end
44	Sept. 16	Zeph 1	Matt 13:1-23
46	Sept. 17	Zeph 2	Matt 13:24-43
49	Sept. 18	Zeph 3	Matt 13:44-end
51	Sept. 19	Hag 1	Matt 14
55	Sept. 20	Hag 2	Matt 15:1-28
58, 60	Sept. 21	Zech 1	Matt 15:29—16:12
63, 64	Sept. 22	Zech 2	Matt 16:13-end
65, 67	Sept. 23	Zech 3	Matt 17:1-23
68:19-36	Sept. 24	Zech 4	Matt 17:24—18:14
69:19-38v	Sept. 25	Zech 5	Matt 18:15-end
70, 72	Sept. 26	Zech 6	Matt 19:1-15
73	Sept. 27	Zech 7	Matt 19:16—20:16
77	Sept. 28	Zech 8	Matt 20:17-end
79, 82	Sept. 29	Zech 9	Matt 21:1-22
78:19-40v	Sept. 30	Zech 10	Matt 21:23-end
80	October 1	Zech 11	Matt 22:1-33
83	October 2	Zech 12	Matt 22:34—23:12
85	October 3	Zech 13	Matt 23:13-end
88	October 4	Zech 14	Matt 24:1-28
89:19-52v	October 5	Mal 1	Matt 24:29-end
91	October 6	Mal 2	Matt 25:1-30
94	October 7	Mal 3	Matt 25:31-end
97, 98	October 8	Mal 4	Matt 26:1-30

The Anglican Rosary

Psalm	Date	Old Testament	New Testament
102	October 9	1 Macc 1 † 1-15,20-25,41-64	Matt 26:31-56
104	October 10	1 Macc 2 † 1-28	Matt 26:57-end
105:23-45v	October 11	2 Macc 6	Matt 27:1-26
106:19-48v	October 12	2 Macc 7	Matt 27:27-56
107:23-43	October 13	2 Macc 8 † 1-29	Matt 27:57—28 end
109	October 14	2 Macc 10 † 1-8,24-38	Mark 1:1-13
113, 114	October 15	1 Macc 7 † 1-6,23-50	Mark 1:14-31
116, 117	October 16	1 Macc 9 † 1-31	Mark 1:32-end
119:25-48	October 17	1 Macc 13 † 1-30,41-42	Mark 2:1-22
119:73-88	October 18	1 Macc 14 † 4-18,35-43	Mark 2:23—3:12
119:105-128	October 19	Isa 1	Mark 3:13-end
119:153-176	October 20	Isa 2	Mark 4:1-34
120, 121	October 21	Isa 3	Mark 4:35—5:20
124, 125, 126	October 22	Isa 4	Mark 5:21-end
129, 130, 131	October 23	Isa 5	Mark 6:1-29
134, 135	October 24	Isa 6	Mark 6:30-end
137, 138	October 25	Isa 7	Mark 7:1-23
141, 142	October 26	Isa 8	Mark 7:24—8:10
143	October 27	Isa 9	Mark 8:11-end
145	October 28	Isa 10	Mark 9:1-29
147	October 29	Isa 11	Mark 9:30-end
149, 150	October 30	Isa 12	Mark 10:1-31
3, 4	October 31	Isa 13	Mark 10:32-end
34	Nov. 1	Isa 14	Rev 19:1-16
7	Nov. 2	Isa 15	Mark 11:1-26
10	Nov. 3	Isa 16	Mark 11:27—12:12
15, 16	Nov. 4	Isa 17	Mark 12:13-34
17	Nov. 5	Isa 18	Mark 12:35—13:13
18:21-50v	Nov. 6	Isa 19	Mark 13:14-end
20, 21	Nov. 7	Isa 20	Mark 14:1-25

Year Two

Psalm	Date	Old Testament	New Testament
23, 24	Nov. 8	Isa 21	Mark 14:26-52
27	Nov. 9	Isa 22	Mark 14:53-end
31	Nov. 10	Isa 23	Mark 15
33	Nov. 11	Isa 24	Mark 16
35	Nov. 12	Isa 25	Luke 1:1-23
38	Nov. 13	Isa 26	Luke 1:24-56
37:19-42v	Nov. 14	Isa 27	Luke 1:57-end
39, 41	Nov. 15	Isa 28	Luke 2:1-21
44	Nov. 16	Isa 29	Luke 2:22-end
46	Nov. 17	Isa 30	Luke 3:1-22
49	Nov. 18	Isa 31	Luke 3:23-end
51	Nov. 19	Isa 32	Luke 4:1-30
55	Nov. 20	Isa 33	Luke 4:31-end
58, 60	Nov. 21	Isa 34	Luke 5:1-16
63, 64	Nov. 22	Isa 35	Luke 5:17-end
65, 67	Nov. 23	Isa 36	Luke 6:1-19
68:19-36	Nov. 24	Isa 37	Luke 6:20-38
69:19-38v	Nov. 25	Isa 38	Luke 6:39—7:10
70, 72	Nov. 26	Isa 39	Luke 7:11-35
73	Nov. 27	Isa 40	Luke 7:36-end
77	Nov. 28	Isa 41	Luke 8:1-21
79, 82	Nov. 29	Isa 42	Luke 8:22-end
78:19-40v	Nov. 30	Isa 43	Luke 9:1-17
80	Dec. 1	Isa 44	Luke 9:18-50
83	Dec. 2	Isa 45	Luke 9:51-end
85	Dec. 3	Isa 46	Luke 10:1-24
88	Dec. 4	Isa 47	Luke 10:25-end
89:19-52v	Dec. 5	Isa 48	Luke 11:1-28
91	Dec. 6	Isa 49	Luke 11:29-end
94	Dec. 7	Isa 50	Luke 12:1-34
97, 98	Dec. 8	Isa 51	Luke 12:35-53
102	Dec. 9	Isa 52	Luke 12:54—13:9
104	Dec. 10	Isa 53	Luke 13:10-end

The Anglican Rosary

Psalm	Date	Old Testament	New Testament
105:23-45v	Dec. 11	Isa 54	Luke 14:1-24
106:19-48v	Dec. 12	Isa 55	Luke 14:25—15:10
107:23-43	Dec. 13	Isa 56	Luke 15:11-end
109	Dec. 14	Isa 57	Luke 16
113, 114	Dec. 15	Isa 58	Luke 17:1-19
116, 117	Dec. 16	Isa 59	Luke 17:20-end
119:25-48	Dec. 17	Isa 60	Luke 18:1-30
119:73-88	Dec. 18	Isa 61	Luke 18:31—19:10
119:105-128	Dec. 19	Isa 62	Luke 19:11-28
119:153-176	Dec. 20	Isa 63	Luke 19:29-end
120, 121	Dec. 21	Isa 64	Luke 20:1-26
124, 125, 126	Dec. 22	Isa 65	Luke 20:27—21:4
129, 130, 131	Dec. 23	Isa 66	Luke 21:5-end
134, 135	Dec. 24	Song of Songs 1	Luke 22:1-38
85, 110	Dec. 25	Song of Songs 2	Luke 2:1-14
137, 138	Dec. 26	Song of Songs 3	Luke 22:39-53
141, 142	Dec. 27	Song of Songs 4	Luke 22:54-end
143	Dec. 28	Song of Songs 5	Luke 23:1-25
145	Dec. 29	Song of Songs 6	Luke:23:26-49
147	Dec. 30	Song of Songs 7	Luke 23:50—24:12
149, 150	Dec. 31	Song of Songs 8	Luke 24:13-end

Acknowledgments

Nobody writes in a vacuum. I am blessed by a community of friends, fellow writers, and family who not only encouraged me but more importantly prayed for me over the years it's taken for this book to come into being.

To my husband, Jack Estes, who inspired me to write. To Carol Raines, whose work with the names of God and the Rosary put us on this trajectory together. To my writing friends, Gay Chambers, Joan Raymond, Donnee Patrese, Janet Skibinski, Carolyn Tilton, Stephanie Apsit, Sandy Moffett and Cydney Haynes—your poignant critiques make me a better writer.

To my daughter, Zoe De Liss, for designing our beautiful press logo, and to fellow writer/designer Cynthia Bermudez for helping with the back cover, I couldn't have put this together without both of you.

To the Women's Bible Study group who went into the trenches with me through prayer, thank you for your encouragement and support—Diane Allen, Kris Eastridge, Sandra Zachary, Merleen Johnson, Nancy Broome, Mary Ann Strong, Donna Starr, Lynn Buckley, Sue Messick, and Caressa Hill.

To Deacon Leslie Arbegast for your spiritual insight and friendship.

And finally, a heartfelt thanks to Kris Eastridge, my workshop helper and travel buddy. Your support and encouragement make our workshop ventures run smoothly and lots of fun. I appreciate your patience and keen observations when I bounce ideas off you.

References

CHAPTER 1 - The Anglican Rosary
Society of St. Francis. *The Anglican Rosary: Contemporary practice of the ancient tradition of prayer and meditation using prayer beads.* Australia. http://www.franciscan.org.au/anglican-rosary/

Millsap, Rick. *The Anglican Rosary.* Reno, NV: Trinity Episcopal Church, 2009. https://dohio.org/EpiscopalDioceseOfOhio/media/EpiscopalDioceseOfOhioMedia/Our%20Diocese/Resources/Documents/Anglican-Rosary.pdf

Sr. Mary Peter. *The History of the Rosary.* Catholicism.org, 2008. https://catholicism.org/rosary-history.html

Doerr, Nan Lewis, and Virginia Stem Owens. *Praying with Beads: Daily Prayers for the Christian Year.* Grand Rapids, MI: Wm. B. Eerdmans Publishing Co., 2007.

Bauman, Lynn C. *The Anglican Rosary.* Telephone, Texas: Praxis, 2003

CHAPTER 2 - The Lord's Prayer
Packer, J.I. *Praying the Lord's Prayer.* Wheaton, IL: Crossway Books, 2007.

Sproul, R.C. *The Prayer of the Lord.* York, PA: Maple Press, 2009.

Wiersbe, Warren W. *On Earth as it is in Heaven: How the Lord's Prayer Teaches Us to Pray More Effectively.* Grand Rapids, Michigan: Bakers Books, 2010.

Wright, N.T. *Into God's Presence: Prayer in the New Testament.* Grand Rapids, MI: Eerdmans, 2001.

CHAPTER 3 - The Daily Office
Texts for Common Prayer. http://anglicanchurch.net/?/main/texts_for_common_prayer

CHAPTER 4 - Holy Mysteries
____. *Pray the Rosary: With Scripture Readings: A Saint Joseph Edition.* New Jersey: Catholic Book Publishing Corp., 2008.

Jansen, Gary. *The Rosary: A Journey to the Beloved.* New York: Madison Park Press, 2006.

Gaitley, Fr. Michael E. *33 Days to Morning Glory: A Do-It-Yourself Retreat in Preparation for Marian Consecration*. Massachusetts: Marian Press, 2011.

Tatro, Rt. Rev. Edward. *The Holy Rosary: From the Independent Canonical Anglican Church Perspective*. Middletown, DE: Independent Canonical Anglican Church, 2016

_____. *Revised Common Lectionary Prayers: Proposed by the Consultation on Common Texts* (Preaching the Revised Common Lectionary). U.S.A.: Augsburg Fortress Publishers, 2002.

CHAPTER 5 - A.C.T.S.
Andrew C. Thompson. *ACTS: 4 Kinds of Prayer for the Christian*. Seedbed.com: September 18, 2016

Biblical and Historical Foundations for Guided Listening Prayer. Evangelism. intervarsity.org

Questions. Christianity.stackexchange.com

CHAPTER 6 - St. Patrick's Breastplate
King of Peace Episcopal Church, Kingsland, Georgia. *Anglican Prayer Beads: A Form of Contemplative Prayer.*
http://www.kingofpeace.org/prayerbeads.htm

CHAPTER 7 - The Way of the Cross
Jansen, Gary. *Station to Station: An Ignatian Journey through the Stations of the Cross*. Chicago, IL: Loyola Press, 2017.

Sheen, Fulton J. *The Way of the Cross*. Staten Island, NY: Society of St. Paul, 2006.

Schumacher, Msgr. M.A. *The Way of the Cross: According to the method of St. Francis of Assisi*. Charlotte, NC: TAN Books, 2012.

Acevedo Butcher, Carmen. *Walking the Walk: (of the Stations of the Cross)*. Waco, TX: The Center for Christian Ethics, Baylor University, 2013.

McKenna, Megan. *The New Stations of the Cross: The Way of the Cross According to Scripture*. New York: Image Books Doubleday, 2003.

CHAPTER 8 - Lectio Divina
Gray, Tim. *Praying Scripture for a Change: An Introduction to Lectio Divina.* West Chester, PA: Ascension Publishing, 2009.

Benner, David G. *Opening to God: Lectio Divina and Life as Prayer.* Downers Grover, IL: InterVarsity Press, 2010.

Langer, Rebecca Bradburn. *Harvest of Righteousness: A Spiritual Discipline of Devotion in the Reformed Tradition.* Louisville, KY: Geneva Press, 1999.

Michael, Chester P., and Marie C. Norrisey. *Prayer and Temperament: Different Prayer Forms For Different Personality Types.* Charlottesville, VA: The Open Door Inc., 2006.

Re, Cindee Snider. *Finding Purpose: Rediscovering Meaning in a Life with Chronic Illness.* Waukesha, WI. Chronic Joy Ministry, 2017.

www.ingramcontent.com/pod-product-compliance
Lightning Source LLC
Chambersburg PA
CBHW052035070526
44584CB00016B/2050